An Analysis of

Seyla Benhabib's

The Rights of Others: Aliens, Residents and Citizens

Burcu Ozcelik
with
Jason Xidias

Published by Macat International Ltd
24:13 Coda Centre, 189 Munster Road, London SW6 6AW.

Distributed exclusively by Routledge
2 Park Square, Milton Park, Abingdon, Oxon OX14 4RN
711 Third Avenue, New York, NY 10017, USA

Routledge is an imprint of the Taylor & Francis Group, an informa business

Printed by CPI Group (UK) Ltd, Croydon CRO 4YY

www.macat.com
info@macat.com

Cataloguing in Publication Data
A catalogue record for this book is available from the British Library.
Library of Congress Cataloguing-in-Publication Data is available upon request.
Cover illustration: Etienne Gilfillan

ISBN 978-1-912304-02-8 (hardback)
ISBN 978-1-912284-73-3 (paperback)
ISBN 978-1-912284-87-0 (e-book)

Notice
The information in this book is designed to orientate readers of the work under analysis,
to elucidate and contextualise its key ideas and themes, and to aid in the development
of critical thinking skills. It is not meant to be used, nor should it be used, as a
substitute for original thinking or in place of original writing or research. References and
notes are provided for informational purposes and their presence does not constitute
endorsement of the information or opinions therein. This book is presented solely for
educational purposes. It is sold on the understanding that the publisher is not engaged
to provide any scholarly advice. The publisher has made every effort to ensure that
this book is accurate and up-to-date, but makes no warranties or representations with
regard to the completeness or reliability of the information it contains. The information
and the opinions provided herein are not guaranteed or warranted to produce particular
results and may not be suitable for students of every ability. The publisher shall not be
liable for any loss, damage or disruption arising from any errors or omissions, or from
the use of this book, including, but not limited to, special, incidental, consequential or
other damages caused, or alleged to have been caused, directly or indirectly, by the
information contained within.

CONTENTS

THE MACAT LIBRARY

The Macat Library is a series of unique academic explorations of seminal works in the humanities and social sciences – books and papers that have had a significant and widely recognised impact on their disciplines. It has been created to serve as much more than just a summary of what lies between the covers of a great book. It illuminates and explores the influences on, ideas of, and impact of that book. Our goal is to offer a learning resource that encourages critical thinking and fosters a better, deeper understanding of important ideas.

Each publication is divided into three Sections: Influences, Ideas, and Impact. Each Section has four Modules. These explore every important facet of the work, and the responses to it.

This Section-Module structure makes a Macat Library book easy to use, but it has another important feature. Because each Macat book is written to the same format, it is possible (and encouraged!) to cross-reference multiple Macat books along the same lines of inquiry or research. This allows the reader to open up interesting interdisciplinary pathways.

To further aid your reading, lists of glossary terms and people mentioned are included at the end of this book (these are indicated by an asterisk [*] throughout) – as well as a list of works cited.

Macat has worked with the University of Cambridge to identify the elements of critical thinking and understand the ways in which six different skills combine to enable effective thinking.
Three allow us to fully understand a problem; three more give us the tools to solve it. Together, these six skills make up the **PACIER** model of critical thinking. They are:

ANALYSIS – understanding how an argument is built
EVALUATION – exploring the strengths and weaknesses of an argument
INTERPRETATION – understanding issues of meaning

CREATIVE THINKING – coming up with new ideas and fresh connections
PROBLEM-SOLVING – producing strong solutions
REASONING – creating strong arguments

To find out more, visit **WWW.MACAT.COM.**

CRITICAL THINKING AND *THE RIGHTS OF OTHERS: ALIENS, RESIDENTS AND CITIZENS*

Primary Critical Thinking Skill: EVALUATION
Secondary Critical Thinking Skill: CREATIVE THINKING

Seyla Benhabib's *The Rights of Others* evaluates the strengths and weaknesses of the scholarship of Immanuel Kant, Hannah Arendt, John Rawls, and Michael Walzer.

Identifying the value in Kant's concept of "the right of universal hospitality," Benhabib critiques his concept of a "temporary right to sojourn." In doing so, the author creates the context for her subsequent claim that all individuals who migrate to the territorial jurisdiction of a new state or host country should be given a path to legal citizenship, or what she calls "just membership." However, to avoid being too idealistic, she also advocates that states should continue to be able to dictate the requirements for citizenship, assuming they always respect the norms of international human rights. Benhabib then draws from Arendt's concept of "the right to have rights," and asserts that no individual should ever be denationalized or stateless. Later, she praises John Rawls's and Michael Walzer's contributions to political philosophy, but firmly claims that they fail to account for the human needs of migrants and refugees, and wrongly portray nation-states as homogenous cultural units whose civic culture and citizenship regimes are threatened by minorities.

In contrast, Benhabib sees diversity as a means of transforming and enriching liberal democratic states and evaluates the work of Jürgen Habermas, a leading proponent of discourse ethics and deliberative democracy. She creatively extends his scholarly contributions in an attempt to reconcile the tensions between universal human rights, minority claims, democratic politics, and the will of nation-states to defend their borders and identities. To make her argument clearer and more tangible to readers, Benhabib provides three case-studies on France and Germany that help bridge the gap between abstract political philosophy and recent debates related to minorities.

ABOUT THE AUTHOR OF THE ORIGINAL WORK

Seyla Benhabib is Eugene Meyer Professor of Political Science and Philosophy at Yale University. She has conducted extensive research on German idealism, Max Weber, the Frankfurt School, and Hannah Arendt, and is one of the most prominent scholars of migration, citizenship, and multiculturalism. She has written numerous important publications, including *The Rights of Others: Aliens, Residents and Citizens*, which won the 2005 Ralph Bunche Award from the American Political Science Association and the Best Book Award from the North American Society for Social Philosophy.

ABOUT THE AUTHORS OF THE ANALYSIS

Dr. Burcu Ozcelik is a Leverhulme Early Career Research Fellow. She received her PhD from the Department of Politics and International Studies at the University of Cambridge, where she was also a Teaching Associate in Conflict, Peacebuilding, and the Politics of the Middle East. Dr Ozcelik is the author of *Kurds Across Borders: Turkey, Iraq and Syria*, and is currently writing a book on women's right-wing political activism in Turkey and the gendered response to the rise of religious nationalism.

Dr Jason Xidias holds a PhD in European Politics from King's College London, where he completed a comparative dissertation on immigration and citizenship in Britain and France. Dr Xidias was also a Visiting Fellow at the University of California, Berkeley. He is currently Lecturer in Political Science at New York University.

ABOUT MACAT

GREAT WORKS FOR CRITICAL THINKING

Macat is focused on making the ideas of the world's great thinkers accessible and comprehensible to everybody, everywhere, in ways that promote the development of enhanced critical thinking skills.

It works with leading academics from the world's top universities to produce new analyses that focus on the ideas and the impact of the most influential works ever written across a wide variety of academic disciplines. Each of the works that sit at the heart of its growing library is an enduring example of great thinking. But by setting them in context – and looking at the influences that shaped their authors, as well as the responses they provoked – Macat encourages readers to look at these classics and game-changers with fresh eyes. Readers learn to think, engage and challenge their ideas, rather than simply accepting them.

'Macat offers an amazing first-of-its-kind tool for interdisciplinary learning and research. Its focus on works that transformed their disciplines and its rigorous approach, drawing on the world's leading experts and educational institutions, opens up a world-class education to anyone.'

Andreas Schleicher,
Director for Education and Skills, Organisation for Economic
Co-operation and Development

'Macat is taking on some of the major challenges in university education ... They have drawn together a strong team of active academics who are producing teaching materials that are novel in the breadth of their approach.'

Prof Lord Broers,
former Vice-Chancellor of the University of Cambridge

'The Macat vision is exceptionally exciting. It focuses upon new modes of learning which analyse and explain seminal texts which have profoundly influenced world thinking and so social and economic development. It promotes the kind of critical thinking which is essential for any society and economy. This is the learning of the future.'

Rt Hon Charles Clarke, former UK Secretary of State for Education

'The Macat analyses provide immediate access to the critical conversation surrounding the books that have shaped their respective discipline, which will make them an invaluable resource to all of those, students and teachers, working in the field.'

Professor William Tronzo, University of California at San Diego

WAYS IN TO THE TEXT

KEY POINTS

- Seyla Benhabib is a renowned professor of political science and philosophy at Yale University.
- *The Rights of Others* examines the tensions between universal human rights,* state sovereignty,* and democratic politics.*
- The text bridges an important gap between abstract political theories on global justice* and case-based research in migration and refugee studies.

Who Is Seyla Benhabib?

Seyla Benhabib was born in Istanbul, Turkey in 1950. She was educated at the American College for Girls in Istanbul before obtaining a grant to study in the United States in 1970. She received her BA in Philosophy from Brandeis University in Massachusetts in 1972 and her PhD in Philosophy from Yale University in Connecticut in 1977.

Benhabib is currently Eugene Meyer Professor of Political Science and Philosophy at Yale University. She is a highly regarded scholar for her research and teaching on European social and political philosophy, and in particular for her expertise on German idealism,* Max Weber,* the Frankfurt School,* and Hannah Arendt.*

Prior to her current position, Benhabib was Director of Yale's program in Ethics, Politics, and Economics (2001-8), and was also Professor of Government at Harvard University (1993-2000). In addition, Benhabib has held many prestigious visiting professorships, including the Spinoza Chair at the University of Amsterdam, the Gauss Lectureship at Princeton University, the John Seeley Memorial Lectureship at Cambridge University, and the Tanner Lectureship at the University of California, Berkeley.

Benhabib is a prolific writer on migration, citizenship, gender, multiculturalism,* and political membership.* Among her most important works are: *Transformations of Citizenship: Dilemmas of the Nation-State in the Era of Globalization* (2000), *The Claims of Culture: Equality and Diversity in the Global Era* (2002), and *The Rights of Others: Aliens, Residents and Citizens* (2004). Her academic work has received several accolades, including the Ernst Bloch Prize* for her contributions to cultural dialogue, the Leopold Lucas Prize* for her scholarship on justice and tolerance, and the Meister Eckhart Prize* for her research on contemporary political and social thought.[1]

What Does *The Rights of Others* Say?

The Rights of Others applies philosophical thinking to the subject of migration and draws attention to a scantly theorized aspect of global justice: political membership. Benhabib makes a series of original arguments, most notably a call for porous borders* to render states more responsive to the rights and needs of migrants, refugees,* and asylum seekers* seeking entry into foreign states. By advocating porous rather than open borders,* Benhabib defends the right of membership to all those who aspire to it once first admittance across a state's territorial borders has taken place, while also recognizing the right of democratic states to regulate the transition from first admission to full membership/legal citizenship. She is greatly inspired by Immanuel Kant,* one of the foremost thinkers of the Enlightenment,* whose moral philosophy resonates with contemporary philosophical justifications of human rights; Georg Wilhelm Friedrich Hegel,* on whose work she based her doctoral dissertation comparing his *concept of right** with the natural rights* tradition; Hannah Arendt's* political thought on denationalization* and statelessness;* and Jürgen Habermas's* ideas on communicative rationality.*

The book is a response to an intellectual environment that is divided between those who defend the necessity of the state-centric international system* and the inevitability of particularistic* cultural and national identities of states, and those, such as Benhabib, who defend a cosmopolitan* alternative in some form. *The Rights of Others* fits into this broader debate through the author's philosophical preoccupation with the tension between adherence to universal human rights on the one hand and the democratic will of self-governing sovereign states on the other. In other words, can cosmopolitanism and democratic self-determination* be reconciled? In Benhabib's understanding, the issue of transnational migration best illustrates this tension, which she calls "the constitutive dilemma at the heart of liberal democracies."*²

Benhabib's cosmopolitan position runs counter to the dominant state-centric system and faces its most serious challenge from Michael Walzer,* who belongs to what Benhabib terms the "decline-of-citizenship school."*³ In general terms, proponents of this view argue that the sovereignty of the nation-state is eroding under the strains of economic globalization* and that the proliferation of human rights norms is causing the deterioration of the institution of citizenship.

Benhabib seeks to mitigate what she sees as a "troubled moment in terms of political culture" where "our fate, as late-modern individuals, is to live caught in the permanent tug of war between the vision of the universal and the attachments to the particular."⁴ She speaks up for the rights of others by challenging contemporary practices of exclusion and asks what immigration, naturalization, and citizenship policies would be compatible with the commitments of liberal democracies to defend human rights.

11

Why Does *The Rights of Others* Matter?

In light of globalization,* immigration, asylum claims, citizenship, multiculturalism, and the rights and duties of non-nationals are key issues of global concern. Benhabib's *The Rights of Others* is a unique theoretical and practical contribution to such ongoing debates. She injects an identifiable human stake in discussions on the worldwide movement of people and urges political philosophers to engage with the real-world consequences of different forms of exclusion suffered by migrants, refugees, and asylum seekers in their host states.

Benhabib is a pre-eminent theorist of the cosmopolitan doctrine or "the concern for the world as if it were one's *polis**" (or community).[5] However, she departs from global justice theorists, such as John Rawls,* who fail to address the empirical realities of migration or question the limits of the nation-state's sovereign prerogative to regulate the movement of peoples across their territorial borders. She sees the real challenge of cosmopolitanism as the reconciliation of universalistic norms with democratic politics. By drawing attention to the challenge of defining political membership, Benhabib engages in a topic that has received too little attention from global justice theorists. The moral and political concern with global interdependencies and the duties that states have to persons beyond their borders is rooted in Benhabib's cosmopolitan commitments. She is highly regarded both within the cosmopolitan school of thought and outside of it, and her ideas have been applied by scholars and practitioners in the fields of immigration and human rights.

Benhabib's clear-cut identification of an inherent tension at the heart of liberal democracies, meaning the commitment to sovereign self-determination on the one hand and adherence to universal human rights claims on the other, is a crucial reason for the enduring influence of the text. Her proposed solutions, which embrace a human right to membership and the notion of porous borders to allow the entry of others* into existing democratic politics, have rendered the text an important, if somewhat contested, scholarly work. She advocates the right of membership to all those who seek it once they have crossed into a state's territorial borders. At the same time, she asserts that democracies have the right to set the rules and requirements of membership, and ultimately, naturalization,* while stipulating that in doing so, international human rights constraints that protect immigrants—such as non-discrimination and the right to due process*—must always be upheld.

The text is original in its approach as well as in its central argument for a right to political membership regardless of a person's nationality. Benhabib's mixed-methods approach, which consists of both a normative-analytical framework and detailed empirical case studies of relevant debates in Europe, bridges a gap between political theory and case-based research in migration and refugee studies. Its impact emanates mainly from its ongoing relevance, but is also due to Benhabib's formulation of unique conceptual tools, such as democratic iterations.* She views iterative acts* as allowing a democratic people which considers itself bound by certain guiding norms and principles to re-appropriate and reinterpret them, thus showing itself to be not only the *subject* but also the *author* of the laws that concern them.

The Rights of Others won the 2005 Ralph Bunche Prize* from the American Political Science Association and the Best Book Award from the North American Society for Social Philosophy. It is an essential read for anyone interested in immigration, refugees, citizenship, multiculturalism, and human rights.

NOTES

1 Yale University, Department of Political Science website, March 18, 2004, accessed March 1, 2018, https://politicalscience.yale.edu/people/seyla-benhabib.

2   Seyla Benhabib, *The Rights of Others: Aliens, Residents and Citizens, John Roberts Seeley Lectures* (Cambridge: Cambridge University Press, 2004), 16.

3   Benhabib, *The Rights of Others*, 115-116, 212.

4   Benhabib, *The Rights of Others*, 16.

5   Benhabib, *The Rights of Others*, 174.

SECTION 1
INFLUENCES

MODULE 1
THE AUTHOR AND THE HISTORICAL CONTEXT

KEY POINTS

- *The Rights of Others* seeks to reconcile the tensions between universal human rights norms, state sovereignty, and democratic politics.

- Seyla Benhabib is a renowned political philosopher and scholar of migration and citizenship.

- Her interest in and passion for these topics is rooted in her family history and upbringing.

Why Read This Text?

Seyla Benhabib's *The Rights of Others: Aliens, Residents and Citizens* makes an important contribution to our understanding of migration, citizenship, and multiculturalism. In the text, she encourages political philosophers to reflect on the humanness of these issues and engage in critical discussions about the different forms of exclusion migrants, refugees, and asylum seekers suffer in western democracies. She critiques political and global justice theorists such as John Rawls and Michael Walzer, asserting that they neglect to address the real-life, human consequences of the movement of people and the pursuit of political membership in their host countries. In so doing, she suggests that we should see the world as one inclusive global community rather than emphasizing collective notions of religious, racial, or ethnic purity, which include some while excluding others. At the same time, she recognizes the great challenge that her cosmopolitan viewpoint presents, which is to reconcile the pursuit of universal human rights with nation-state* sovereignty and democratic politics. This focus on

> **❝** My ancestors are Sephardic Jews who fled Spain in 1492 when the Inquisition was forcing Jews to convert, or decimating them, forcing them to go underground. At the time, the Ottoman Empire had a policy of giving refuge to the Jewish community escaping from Spain. **❞**
>
> Seyla Benhabib, "Philosophical Iterations, Cosmopolitanism, and the 'Right to Rights,' Conversation with Seyla Benhabib"

political membership differentiates her work from the aforementioned scholars, as well as other political theorists, such as Thomas Pogge* and Charles Beitz,* and thus makes an original scholarly and practical contribution. In particular, by linking her academic framework to specific, contemporary examples concerning minority rights in France and Germany, she narrows the gap between abstract philosophy and political debates and policies.

In her concluding section, Benhabib aims to reconcile universal human rights with state sovereignty and democratic politics. She does this by advocating for porous borders, meaning she supports the right of membership of all those who seek to obtain it after having been admitted into a state's territorial borders. At the same, she argues that states should maintain their sovereign right to establish the conditions by which these individuals would transition from aliens* to citizens, as long as they always respect international human rights norms.[1]

The Rights of Others is a highly regarded text in the disciplines of Political Science and Philosophy. Due to the increasing numbers of migrants and refugees and the heated debates concerning their reception and integration,[2] Benhabib's work on the tensions between borders, politics, and rights claims continues to be a key point of reference for scholars and practitioners.

Author's Life

Seyla Benhabib was born in Turkey in 1950. She completed her secondary education at the American College for Girls in Istanbul before accepting a grant to study a BA in Philosophy at Brandeis University in 1970. Upon finishing her undergraduate degree, she went on to study an MA and PhD in Philosophy at Yale University.

Benhabib wrote her PhD dissertation on G.W.F. Hegel's *Philosophy of Right*, which deals with the relationships between morality, legality, and ethics. This, along with her in-depth study of the works of Immanuel Kant and Hannah Arendt lay the foundation for the rest of her academic career: "For me, the issue starting already in that work [Hegel's *Philosophy of Right*] was how to reconcile universalistic principles of human rights, autonomy, and freedom with our concrete particular identity as members of certain human communities divided by language, by ethnicity, by religion."[3]

Upon graduating, Benhabib worked as an academic at several institutions, including Harvard University, Boston University, and the New School for Social Research. In 2001, she became the Director of Yale's program in Ethics, Politics, and Economics, a position which she held until 2008. Since then, Benhabib has been the Eugene Meyer Professor of Political Science and Philosophy at the same institution. She is widely considered to be one of the foremost scholars on migration, citizenship, multiculturalism, and human rights.

Author's Background

Seyla Benhabib's passion for migration, citizenship, multiculturalism, and human rights is rooted in her family history. Her ancestors were Sephardic Jews,* who were forced into exile in 1492 due to the Spanish Inquisition.* Faced with the options of converting to Christianity* or death, her family managed to escape to what is Turkey today. At the time, the Ottoman Empire,* which was a multi-ethnic and multicultural system, had an open, tolerant policy toward exiled Jews.

She described the impact of her family history on her work as follows:"It makes me aware of the fragility of good political institutions. I never take them for granted. I am always attentive to the ways in which, particularly, collective ideologies of purity—be it religious purity, racial purity, or national purity—can go wrong."[4]

In addition, in her work, Benhabib emphasized the importance of her multicultural upbringing in Turkey. As she put it, "Istanbul was a city in which you ... could encounter many neighborhoods, varieties of food and taste." Furthermore, her home and school environments were very diverse: her mother attended a French primary school and an Italian secondary school, and Benhabib attended English-speaking schools throughout her childhood and adolescence. She recalled interacting at home in a mixture of Turkish, Ladino,* French, and Italian, and mingling at school with Turks, Greeks, and Armenians, among others. As such, she always felt that she had one foot in the East and another in the West, leading to her self-identification as cosmopolitan, rather than an ethnic Turk.[5] This open, worldly profile is tangible in all her scholarship.

Finally, it is important to note that Benhabib's interest in political philosophy emanated from the diverse social and political protests of the 1960s in the United States and Europe. In particular, she recalled conversing with American teachers at her school in Istanbul who had evaded the Vietnam War draft.* "The news of the Vietnam War was what we talked about during our lunch hours," she observed. "I remember seeing those pictures of people who had been exposed to napalm bombing, etc., and there was a speedy process of politicization. So there was the Vietnam War, there was the student movement, and in Turkey, in particular, there was the emergence of an independent left, a very significant mobilization among the workers. History was knocking at the door, and if you were a thoughtful or reflective person, you had to focus on the political issues."[6] This historical context shaped Benhabib's future decision to study Politics and Philosophy at Brandeis University, and then at Yale University.

NOTES

1   Seyla Benhabib, *The Rights of Others: Aliens, Residents and Citizens, John Roberts Seeley Lectures* (Cambridge: Cambridge University Press, 2004), 42.

2   Benhabib, *The Rights of Others*, 5.

3   Harry Kreisler, "Philosophical Iterations, Cosmopolitanism, and the 'Right to Rights,' Conversation with Seyla Benhabib," *Institute of International Studies, UC Berkeley*, March 18, 2004, accessed March 1, 2018, http://globetrotter.berkeley.edu/people4/Benhabib/benhabib-con2.html.

4   Kreisler, "Philosophical Iterations, Cosmopolitanism, and the 'Right to Rights.'"

5   Kreisler, "Philosophical Iterations, Cosmopolitanism, and the 'Right to Rights.'"

6   Kreisler, "Philosophical Iterations, Cosmopolitanism, and the 'Right to Rights.'"

MODULE 2
ACADEMIC CONTEXT

KEY POINTS

- Debates regarding global justice in relation to human rights, state sovereignty, and democratic politics can be divided into two camps.
- The first camp consists of proponents of the "decline-of-citizenship" perspective; the second is made up of different cosmopolitan strands.
- *The Rights of Others* builds on the work of Immanuel Kant, Hannah Arendt, John Rawls, and Michael Walzer in an attempt to reconcile this tension.

The Work in its Context

Seyla Benhabib's *The Rights of Others: Aliens, Residents and Citizens* addresses the contradictions and tensions between human rights and sovereignty, a topic of debate that can be traced back to the classical liberal period,* or even to antiquity.* Great minds such as Thomas Hobbes,* John Locke,* and Jean-Jacques Rousseau* built on the ideas of Aristotle,* Plato,* and others, in an attempt to grapple with this complex relationship.

In a more modern context, scholarly discussions can broadly be divided into two camps: the first is what Seyla Benhabib denominated the "decline-of-citizenship school."[1] Proponents of this perspective, notably Michael Walzer, argued that economic globalization was eroding nation-state sovereignty and the proliferation of international human rights norms was undermining national citizenship. They considered migrants, refugees, and asylum seekers to be a threat to national communities, and therefore advocate that nation-states

> **❝** Kant leaves unexplained the philosophical and political step that could lead from the right of temporary sojourn to the right of membership. **❞**
>
> Seyla Benhabib, *The Rights of Others*

exercise their self-determination or right to sovereignty in order to protect their borders and identities.

The second camp was made up of different strands of cosmopolitanism. Proponents of this school of thought, such as Joseph Carens* and Benhabib, defend openness and tolerance against nationalism* and exclusion. Cosmopolitanism's ethical orientation essentially maintains that there are moral obligations owed to all human beings based solely on our humanity. This notion of common humanity transcends territorial borders and translates ethically into an idea of shared moral duties toward others. Cosmopolitanism is universal in its scope, holding that the moral standing of all humans applies to everyone equally and assumes that all individuals are "moral and political agencies in a world society."[2] In the case of migrants, refugees, and asylum seekers, this either means having *open* (Carens) or *porous* borders (Benhabib). In both incarnations, it seeks to ensure that these individuals have a path to full membership in their host communities.

Overview of the Field

The Rights of Others addressed tensions between transnational migration, universal human rights, state sovereignty, and democratic politics. Benhabib described these as "the constitutive dilemma at the heart of liberal democracies."[3] More specifically, she examined the stark divide between the "decline-of-citizenship" and cosmopolitan camps. Eventually, she attempted to reconcile this debate through, on the one hand, advocating porous borders;

and, on the other, asserting that sovereign states should maintain the authority to dictate their own paths to full citizenship, as long as they adhere to international human rights law.[4]

Benhabib's advocacy for cosmopolitanism and her attempt to reconcile these two camps is aimed at a number of political theorists, the two most prominent of which are Rawls and Walzer. Benhabib argued that these renowned scholars addressed topics like ethics and justice but ignored the human needs of transnational migrants, refugees, and asylum seekers. She pointed out that they portrayed them as a threat to—or dilution of—an already attained, static community of solidarity rather than a source of potential transformation and enrichment.[5] As a critique, she claimed, "collective identities of liberal democracies have never been characterized by the degree of cohesiveness and culture-centeredness that these theorists attribute to them."[6] Rather, she asserted that national communities were ever-evolving and constituted through social and political conflicts and compromises. Furthermore, she encouraged political philosophers and multicultural, democratic nations to engage in continual argument, deliberation, and exchange in order to shape mutually acceptable reconciliations between universal human rights and the will of states to dictate the conditions of citizenship. This should take into account class, gender, ethnicity, and religion and critically address power hierarchies and structures of oppression.

Academic Influences

Benhabib specializes in European—particularly German—political thought. Immanuel Kant, Georg Wilhelm Friedrich Hegel, and Jürgen Habermas, among other scholars, have had a major influence on her work. Benhabib has also written extensively on issues of gender, culture, and identity; in these areas, thinkers such as Hannah Arendt, Judith Shklar,* and Hanna Pitkin* have inspired her.

In *The Rights of Others*, Benhabib examined Kant's doctrine of cosmopolitan right by focusing on the Third Article of his 1795 essay, "Perpetual Peace." This concerned Kant's notion of the right of universal hospitality through which he defended "the right of a stranger not to be treated as an enemy when he arrives in a foreign land."[7] Furthermore, Kant developed the "temporary right to sojourn" (*besuchsrecht*). For Kant, this entails a claim by a foreigner to temporary residency in another state that cannot be refused, if such refusal would result in their "destruction" (*untergang*), or pose a danger to the claimant's life or freedom. Benhabib argued that "Kant set the terms which still guide our thinking on refugee and asylum claims on the one hand, and immigration on the other."[8]

Benhabib then asserted that Kant's formulation was more minimal than she found morally defensible, since he advocated for the right of visitation but not a right of long-term stay. Kant argued that permanence was a special privilege which sovereign states could award to certain foreigners but that they had no moral obligation to do so.[9] Against this position, Benhabib made the case that nations have a moral obligation to receive refugees and argued that, once migrants and asylum seekers pass a country's borders, they should be provided with a path to citizenship or full membership in their national communities. Benhabib considered this a fundamental right held by all persons based on our common condition of humanity.

NOTES

1   Seyla Benhabib, *The Rights of Others: Aliens, Residents and Citizens, John Roberts Seeley Lectures* (Cambridge: Cambridge University Press, 2004), 211.

2   Benhabib, *The Rights of Others*, 92.

3   Benhabib, *The Rights of Others*, 2.

4   Benhabib, *The Rights of Others*, 42.

5   Benhabib, *The Rights of Others*, 173.

6   Benhabib, *The Rights of Others*, 173.

7   Benhabib, *The Rights of Others*, 27.

8   Benhabib, *The Rights of Others*, 21.

9   Benhabib, *The Rights of Others*, 28.

MODULE 3
THE PROBLEM

KEY POINTS

- *The Rights of Others* explores the access of immigrants and asylum seekers to political membership in liberal democracies.

- The text challenges "decline-of-citizenship" scholars who fail to address the different forms of exclusion minorities face.

- Benhabib presents a cosmopolitan framework that seeks to mitigate the tensions between human rights, state sovereignty, and democratic politics.

Core Question

Seyla Benhabib's *The Rights of Others: Aliens, Residents and Citizens* explores the philosophical and institutional meaning of political membership in liberal democratic states. It does this through an examination of the practices and principles that determine how others—meaning immigrants, refugees, and asylum seekers—are incorporated into existing polities in a world of increasingly de-territorialized* politics.

Although the transnational movement of people across borders is not a new phenomenon, recent globalization has borne a set of new challenges upon the self-understanding of liberal democracies at an accelerated pace. It has also rendered decisions about who constitutes the *demos** a complex task in increasingly multi-ethnic and multicultural polities. Meanwhile, international human rights regimes—such as the Geneva Convention (1949)* and its subsequent protocols—have made the rights of others a global concern with

> ❝ By *political membership*, I mean the principles and practices for incorporating aliens and strangers, immigrants and newcomers, refugees and asylum seekers, into existing polities. ❞
>
> Seyla Benhabib, *The Rights of Others*

interrelated policy, regulative, and ethical challenges. By drawing attention to the transformation of conventional conceptions of national citizenship, territoriality, democratic voice, and representation in a globalizing world, Benhabib engaged in a topic that has received minimal attention from global justice theorists. The key question she posed was: in an era of globalization, how can people reconcile universal human rights claims, declining state sovereignty, weakened citizenship regimes, and democratic politics? She considered this question to be of the utmost importance due to the ongoing politicization of migrant and refugee movements globally and the exclusion that many minorities face.

The Participants

The Rights of Others contributed to prevailing debates between "decline-of-citizenship" theorists and political philosophers of global justice and cosmopolitanism. The debate rests between those who defend the state-centric international system versus some form of cosmopolitan alternative.

The text engaged with and challenged the ideas of renowned scholars such as John Rawls and Michael Walzer. More specifically, Benhabib's concept of "cosmopolitan federalism"* intends to mitigate the tension between those who condemn the closed-door policies of wealthy nations and those who insist that migrations pose a threat to the values and identities of liberal democracies.[1] While other scholars such as Thomas Pogge* and Charles Beitz* have explored the possibility of a new kind of cosmopolitan politics, Benhabib focused specifically on migration and asylum seekers. She advanced a clear-cut articulation of the notion of Kantian cosmopolitan federalism, which sought to better reflect and accommodate aspects of the current global political landscape.

Benhabib presented a careful disaggregation of the main philosophical arguments of Kant, Hannah Arendt, and John Rawls before concluding that none go far enough to justify a human right to just membership.* For example, while Arendt saw citizenship as the prime guarantor of a person's human rights, Benhabib asserted that the real challenge was to develop an "international regime that decouples the right to have rights from one's nationality status."[2]

The Contemporary Debate

Benhabib entered the debate on the premise that "political membership—the conditions of entry and exit into societies—has rarely been considered an important aspect of theories of domestic and international justice."[3] Benhabib's cosmopolitan intellectual tradition maintains that "decline-of-citizenship" theorists, such as Michael Walzer, overestimated the cohesion of communities and promoted an idealized model of citizenship based on ethno-cultural affinities, shared language, and cultural heritages. The cosmopolitan worldview, in contrast, recognized that polities are not homogenous units but instead are internally fractured and "negotiate the terms of their own collective identities at the site of migration debates."[4] Furthermore, it asserted that most migrants contribute economically to nation-states and strengthen their political culture, with Benhabib citing the United States as an example.[5]

The debate clearly has no easy answers. Benhabib's solution was neither the end of the state system nor a radical call for world citizenship.* Her intellectual position took account of the decline-of-citizenship theorists' concerns regarding the transformations of citizenship in contemporary democracies and the legitimacy of boundaries, but she found that scholars like Walzer wrongly suggested that "aliens" threaten or dilute an already attained community of solidarity.

Ultimately, Benhabib sought to mediate the tensions between international human rights norms and the desire of states to defend their borders and "national values and identities."[6] She did this through what she called "iterative processes," which consisted of democratic activism, engagement, and debate at different levels of society (i.e., locally, regionally, nationally, and within the European Union).[7] Scholars dealing with similar issues, such as Jürgen Habermas, have praised Benhabib's original philosophical approach and contributions.[8] However, some critics, like Michael Walzer, have called some of her arguments into question, arguing that the application of such a right to citizenship was implausible in the real world.[9]

NOTES

1   Seyla Benhabib, *The Rights of Others: Aliens, Residents and Citizens, John Roberts Seeley Lectures* (Cambridge: Cambridge University Press, 2004), 2–3, 176, 213.

2   Benhabib, *The Rights of Others*, 68.

3   Benhabib, *The Rights of Others*, 74.

4   Benhabib, *The Rights of Others*, 127.

5   Benhabib, *The Rights of Others*, 89.

6   Benhabib, *The Rights of Others*, 120.

7   Benhabib, *The Rights of Others*, 24.

8   Jürgen Habermas, "Further reflections on the public sphere,' in *Habermas and the Public Sphere*, ed. Craig Calhoun (Cambridge, MA: MIT Press, 1993), 421-462.

9   Michael Walzer, "In Response: Support for Modesty and the Nation-State," *Responsive Community* 11/2 (2001): 28-31.

MODULE 4
THE AUTHOR'S CONTRIBUTION

KEY POINTS

- *The Rights of Others* makes a theoretical and practical contribution to our understanding of political membership in democratic societies.

- Seyla Benhabib presents a potential middle ground between cosmopolitans and "decline-of-citizenship" theorists.

- The text advocates the use of discourse ethics* and deliberative democracy* in order to achieve greater global justice.

Author's Aims

Seyla Benhabib's *The Rights of Others: Aliens, Residents and Citizens* aimed to make a theoretically and empirically substantiated argument for re-conceptualizing the boundaries of political membership in liberal democracies. She intended to make a persuasive case for recognizing the right to membership as a human right. She did so from a claim to cosmopolitan federalism in the tradition of Immanuel Kant, who drew a distinction between a world government and a world federation. Kant argued that whereas the former would breed a "soulless despotism," the latter would permit the exercise of citizenship within bounded communities.[1]

Benhabib's vision of cosmopolitan federalism acknowledged the enduring significance of a person's membership within a bounded community, while also recognizing the need for other forms of "democratic attachment" (e.g., at the subnational* or supranational* levels), which may go beyond existing state structures. She viewed

> ❝ Transnational migrations, and the constitutional as well as policy issues suggested by the movement of peoples across state borders, are central to interstate relations and therefore to a normative theory of global justice. ❞
> Seyla Benhabib, *The Rights of Others*

membership in bounded communities, which may be smaller or larger than territorially defined nation-states, as crucial.[2] Benhabib attempted to reconcile the tension between the universal norm of equality of all persons versus real equality being embedded in communities, where such norms may not be fully realized for all persons equally. She argued, "every society has to have institutions enabling 'strangers,' the 'others,' to become members."[3] She proposed steps to fully achieve such a right to membership for migrants, refugees, and asylum seekers at the national level while still defending the state's sovereign right to set reasonable rules for admission and integration into its polity. Through these intentions and her use of actual debates in France and Germany, she bridged the gap between abstract philosophy on morality, ethics, and justice and tangible cases of exclusion involving minorities.

Approach
Benhabib's subsequent arguments follow the work's overall intent and form a logical plan. The author outlined the virtues and limitations of the key ideas articulated by prominent global justice theorists in relation to trans-border migration and citizenship rights. Her account of Kant's doctrine of temporary universal hospitality, Hannah Arendt's defense of the "right to have rights,"[4] and John Rawls's *The Law of Peoples* sets the stage for her own conceptualization of the human right of non-citizens to full membership in their host countries.

Hannah Arendt's *The Origins of Totalitarianism* (1951) asserted that all individuals, regardless of nationality, have "the right to have rights."[5] She wrote this in response to Jews being stripped of their citizenship rights, and therefore human rights, in different European contexts in the nineteenth and twentieth centuries. The right to have rights entailed belonging to a state community in which they could freely express their opinions and be judged by them, rather than being judged by their birth characteristics. Arendt argued that all nations must enshrine this civic conception of polity into their democratic constitutions, though she acknowledged that this would never completely eradicate the distinctions between insiders and outsiders.[6] In Benhabib's analysis, she emphasized the shortcomings of Kant's and Arendt's key concepts: "Arendt could not base 'the right to have rights,' i.e., to be recognized as a member of some organized human community, upon some further philosophical principle." And, [Arendt and Kant] "believe that exclusionary territorial control is an unchecked sovereign privilege which cannot be limited or trumped by other norms and institutions."[7]

In order to develop her concept of cosmopolitan federalism, Benhabib also scrutinized John Rawls's vision of society in *Theory of Justice* (1971) and *Political Liberalism* (1993), claiming that it was too state centric, and therefore did not deal with the realities of transnational migration. Rawls, like Walzer, defended closed and well-guarded borders in order to safeguard what he perceived as already attained cohesive communities grounded in a strong rule of law and civic culture. He treated societies or nations as static rather than continually in motion, and falsely assumed that the good fortunes of developed societies are wholly a consequence of their superior institutions and morality. This nationalistic approach obscured capitalistic* and imperialistic* oppression and exploitation based on class, gender, ethnicity, religion, etc. Furthermore, Benhabib asserted that Rawls concept of redistributive justice* (i.e., redistributing resources from richer to poorer countries to lessen inequalities and reduce the outflow of migration) was too limited. Building on the scholarship of Charles Beitz (1979) and Thomas Pogge (2002), Benhabib postulated that redistributive justice must be combined with just membership.[8]

Contribution in Context

Benhabib examined political membership from the point of view of discourse ethics and deliberative democracy. In doing so, she built on her previous work and that of Jürgen Habermas, applying these concepts specifically to the themes of inclusion and exclusion. She defined discourse ethics as follows: "only those norms and normative institutional arrangements are valid which can be agreed to by all concerned under special argumentation situations named discourses."[9] Furthermore, she asserted that deliberative democracy should always be based on universal moral respect and egalitarian reciprocity. By universal respect, she meant that all individuals capable of speech and action should have the right to be equal participants in dialogue. She described this as follows: "I have a moral obligation to justify my actions with reasons to this individual or to the representatives of this being. I respect the moral worth of the other by recognizing that I must provide them with a justification for my actions."[10]

This approach sought to mitigate morality, ethics, and politics. More specifically, it aimed to reconcile immigration, asylum claims, border control, naturalization, and citizenship with moral, ethical, and constitutional values.

The text concluded that some practices of democratic closure are more justifiable than others but that all policies are open to challenge and reinterpretation. Thus, there is an essential process of deliberation and learning involved. Finally, she asserted that cosmopolitanism, to which she adhered, was a post-national,* moral project of solidarity that must transcend existing state boundaries and the exclusionary practices of nationalism.

Benhabib fulfilled her overall objective, putting forward an impassioned argument in defense of the right to just membership and setting out in clear terms what this might entail in liberal democracies. She called for not open but porous borders; an injunction against permanent alienage; and the right to citizenship on the part of aliens who have met certain conditions established by the host state. Through carefully constructed argumentation, Benhabib presented the theoretical possibility of mediating the friction between cosmopolitans who condemn the closed-door policies of wealthy nations and other theorists, such as Rawls and Walzer, who suggest that worldwide migrations pose a threat to liberal-democratic values and "national cultures."[11]

NOTES

1   Immanuel Kant, "Perpetual Peace," in *On History*, ed. Lewis White Beck (Indianapolis and New York: Library of Liberal Arts, [1795] 1957); Seyla Benhabib, *The Rights of Others: Aliens, Residents and Citizens, John Roberts Seeley Lectures* (Cambridge: Cambridge University Press, 2004), 96.

2   Benhabib, *The Rights of Others*, 2–3, 176, 213.

3   Deniz Utlu, "Interview with Seyla Benhabib: The Guest Is Always a Fellow Citizen," October 26, 2009, accessed February 19, 2018, http://en.qantara.de/The-Guest-is-Always-a-Fellow-Citizen/9613c9712i1p223/index.html.

4   Hannah Arendt, *The Origins of Totalitarianism* (New York: Harcourt, Brace and Jovanovich, [1951] 1968).

5   Benhabib, *The Rights of Others*, 65.

6   Benhabib, *The Rights of Others*, 65.

7   Benhabib, *The Rights of Others*, 65-7.

8   Benhabib, *The Rights of Others*, 72-100.

9   Benhabib, *The Rights of Others*, 13.

10 Benhabib, *The Rights of Others*, 14.

11 Benhabib, *The Rights of Others*, 173.

SECTION 2
IDEAS

MODULE 5
MAIN IDEAS

KEY POINTS

- The main themes in *The Rights of Others* are migration, citizenship, state sovereignty, and democratic politics.

- Benhabib proposes cosmopolitan federalism as a potential answer to the tensions between these main themes.

- The author defines four key concepts central to her analysis: other, cosmopolitanism, democratic iterations, and jurisgenerative politics.*

Key Themes

Seyla Benhabib's *The Rights of Others: Aliens, Residents and Citizens* engaged with contemporary debates around political membership in Europe and the United States and the cross-border movement of migrants, refugees, and asylum seekers. The transformations of the institution of citizenship and the changing nature of state sovereignty in relation to globalization and international human rights regimes were also key concerns of the text.

Benhabib described what she called the *paradox of democratic legitimacy*: "Transnational migrations bring to the fore the constitutive dilemma at the heart of liberal democracies: between sovereign self-determination claims on the one hand and adherence to universal human rights principles on the other."[1]

Benhabib then emphasized the need to "decriminalize" migration and refugee movements by treating all persons—regardless of birth characteristics (ethnicity, race, etc.)—with morality and dignity. She asserted that crossing borders and residing in different polities must not be viewed in a negative light; rather, it should be seen as an expression

> ❝ The new politics of membership is about negotiating this complex relationship between the rights of full membership, democratic voice, and territorial residence. ❞
>
> Seyla Benhabib, *The Rights of Others*

of human freedom and an opportunity for human exchange. Extending the ideas of Immanuel Kant and Jürgen Habermas, she advocated for a cosmopolitan notion of universal, permanent hospitality, the conditions of which all individuals concerned deliberate and decide. In advocating this approach, Benhabib asserts that the identity of a nation is an ongoing process of transformation and heterogeneity, not a static, homogeneous community that must defensively protect itself against change.[2]

Finally, Benhabib advocated for the reception of refugees and a path to citizenship for all migrants who enter into a state different from their home country and meet the conditions established by that state for naturalization (e.g. a citizenship test, etc.). She denominated this as "porous borders" or "post-national solidarity" and stressed the need for a constitutional prohibition of denaturalization* or stripping individuals of citizenship rights.[3]

Exploring the Ideas

Initially, Benhabib set the broad theoretical framework of *The Rights of Others* against the backdrop of what she saw as the "paradox of democratic legitimacy" that lies at the heart of liberal democracies.[4] The paradox was that states agree to bind their will by a set of universal human rights principles, while still asserting their territorially bound sovereignty. She argued that while the paradox can never be fully resolved, "its impact can be mitigated through a renegotiation and reiteration between the dual commitments to human rights and sovereign self-determination."[5] Benhabib viewed the issue of immigrants' political membership rights as "a crucial test for the moral conscience as well as political reflexivity of liberal democracies."[6]

She proceeded along this discursive path by first arguing that the interdependence of peoples in a global order was an empirical reality and a norm in human history rather than an exception. To support this claim, she attempted to dispel certain foundational myths which she argued serve as the basis of democratic rule, such as the view that polities are homogeneous and territorially self-sufficient or closed societies. She proposes pluralism as a morally defensible alternative and one which would recognize the "multiple and dynamic ties, interactions and crisscrossings of peoples."[7]

Benhabib presented a theoretic grounding of rights claims which led her to argue that the right to membership was a human right. The opposite of this right to membership in her view was the interdiction against denaturalization or loss of membership. Benhabib sought to support her position through her subsequent institutional-sociological analysis of the transformations of the institution of citizenship in Europe. She pointed to what she called the "disaggregation of citizenship"[8] and provided compelling evidence for how the traditional model of citizenship was coming apart in the European Union,* given how the rights of citizens of member countries and those of third-country nationals* were delineated within a patchwork of local, national, and supranational rights regimes.[9] For example, French citizens living in Germany can vote in municipal elections and run as a local candidate for European parliamentary elections.

In the final stages of her analysis, Benhabib turned to the position she characterized as cosmopolitan federalism, which she referred to several times throughout the text. This concept, according to Benhabib, made it possible to negotiate "between the norms of international law and the actions of individual democratic legislatures" by using what she calls "democratic iterations." She proposed that states "decriminalize the worldwide movement of peoples, and treat each person, whatever his or her political citizenship status, in accordance with the dignity of moral personhood."[10]

Language and Expression

Benhabib defined several concepts that were central to her analysis, including the other, cosmopolitanism, democratic iterations, and jurisgenerative politics.*

The term other is widely used in the social sciences to denote persons or groups which are generally viewed as different from the culture, ethnicity, language, or ideology of the majority in any given society. Such processes of othering between "us" and "them" has often meant that societies create rules of membership for those whom they seek to subordinate, control, or exclude. The idea of the other is largely attributed to the philosopher Emmanuel Levinas* and was subsequently expanded upon by numerous thinkers. Perhaps the best example is Edward Said,* who applied the concept of othering in his well-known book *Orientalism* (1978) to better understand Western perceptions and formulations of Eastern cultures.[11] Benhabib used the term other to defend the rights of minorities and challenge their perpetual otherness or exclusion in liberal democratic states.

Benhabib is a proponent of cosmopolitanism, a moral ideal and political philosophy concerned with living in one shared world with others. She argued for the recognition of a right to political membership for all persons regardless of their citizenship status. By membership, Benhabib meant the rules and rituals of entry, access, belonging, and privilege employed by the nation-state to define the political boundaries between citizens and non-citizens. Benhabib looked at the concept of national citizenship, the nation-state's primary instrument deployed to regulate the rules of membership.

Two related ideas that are central to Benhabib's conceptual scheme are those of democratic iterations and jurisgenerative politics. Benhabib modified the term iteration from Jacques Derrida's* work (1982; 1991) on the philosophy of language. Democratic iterations describe the ways in which linguistic, cultural, legal, and political concepts or norms are re-signified, transformed, and reinterpreted to take on new meanings. Jurisgenerative politics is a legal concept that was first identified by Robert Cover (1983).* It refers to iterative acts through which a democratic people shows itself to be not only the subject but also the author of the laws that concern them.[12]

NOTES

1 Seyla Benhabib, *The Rights of Others: Aliens, Residents and Citizens, John Roberts Seeley Lectures* (Cambridge: Cambridge University Press, 2004), 2.

2 Benhabib, *The Rights of Others*, 177.

3 Benhabib, *The Rights of Others*, 3, 17.

4 Benhabib, *The Rights of Others*, 2.

5 Benhabib, *The Rights of Others*, 47.

6 Benhabib, *The Rights of Others*, 178.

7 Benhabib, *The Rights of Others*, 93.

8 Benhabib, *The Rights of Others*, 21.

9 Benhabib, *The Rights of Others*, 146.

10 Benhabib, *The Rights of Others*, 177.

11 Edward Said, *Orientalism* (New York: Pantheon, 1978).

12 Benhabib, *The Rights of Others*, 181.

MODULE 6
SECONDARY IDEAS

KEY POINTS

- Seyla Benhabib rejects the idea that European Union countries have self-contained, static national identities.
- She argues that their political communities are pluralistic, that identity and rights are internally contested, and that there is a great interdependence among nations.
- One of the shortcomings of *The Rights of Others* is that it overlooks the different forms of exclusion that minorities suffer after they become citizens.

Other Ideas

Given the importance of Seyla Benhabib's defense of porous borders to her vision of cosmopolitan justice in *The Rights of Others: Aliens, Residents and Citizens*, it is worthwhile to explain in greater depth why she made such a claim. An important secondary idea in the text is Benhabib's call to dispel what she calls "constitutive illusions" that serve as the basis of democratic rule.[1] These illusions are the homogeneity of the people and territorial self-sufficiency. She argued that a vision of unitary, self-contained states is outdated and that global interdependencies among states and peoples are now the norm and not the exception. She rejected the idealized depiction of a culturally homogenous citizenry and defends instead the reality that political communities in liberal democratic states are pluralist and internally contested.

In making this claim, Benhabib critiqued Michael Walzer's *Spheres of Justice* (1983) and his subsequent work at different points in the text, arguing that he "conflates ethical and political integration, in that he views the liberal–democratic state as a holistic cultural and ethical

> **‘‘** Walzer is skeptical, or maybe better still, agnostic about universal human rights claims. **’’**
>
> Seyla Benhabib, *The Rights of Others*

entity."[2] In particular, she focused on and challenged Walzer's claim that the "distinctiveness of cultures and groups depends upon closure and, without it, cannot be conceived as a stable feature of human life."[3] This delineation paved the way for her concept of cosmopolitan federalism, which sought to mitigate the tensions between universal human rights norms and the desire of nation-states to safeguard their sovereignty.

Exploring the Ideas

Benhabib identified a tension in international law. On one hand, the human right of individuals to move across borders whether for economic, personal, or professional reasons or to seek asylum and refuge is guaranteed in Articles 13 and 14 of the 1948 *Universal Declaration of Human Rights*.[4]* On the other hand, she explained how Article 21 of the declaration recognized a basic right to self-government, stipulating that "the will of the people shall be the basis of the authority of government."[5] As a result, "under the current regime of states, that fundamental right includes control over borders as well as determining *who* is to be a citizen as distinguished from a resident or an alien."[6] Essentially, this meant that while the liberal tradition recognizes the right to leave one's country of origin as a basic human right, it does not see a corresponding right on the part of any nation-state to accept the migrant into their polity.[7]

Benhabib proposed the idea of porous borders as a way of mediating between a person's freedom of movement and the state's right to determine its admittance policies. She defended the "right of self-governing communities to determine *certain* conditions of entry as well as membership,"[8] for example, for the purposes of protecting indigenous labor markets. In this way, she rejected the charge that states must, without exception, formally admit into their political communities all persons who achieve entry across national borders and who, pursuant to entry, seek membership rights and entitlements. But she was adamant that "once first admittance occurs, membership ought to be open to all in principle who aspire to it, including to the undocumented whose status can be legalized or regularized."[9] Benhabib stipulated that in doing so, international human rights constraints that protect immigrants—such as non-discrimination and the right to due process—must be upheld.

Overlooked

The Rights of Others has been thoroughly examined from several angles by political philosophers, immigration advocates, legal theorists, and academics. The rigorous examination of the ideas undergirding Benhabib's conceptual scheme has left few, if any, stones unturned, and most of her ideas have been unpacked, reconsidered, and recast in various cultural, empirical, and theoretical contexts.

It may be useful to reflect on what Benhabib overlooked when conceiving of a right to just membership. What membership essentially meant for Benhabib was the right of immigrants to permanent residence, equal protection, and, eventually, to full citizenship in democratic states. However, Benhabib neglected to consider the constraints imposed upon those persons who hold citizenship status, but are nonetheless restricted in their ability to participate fully in what she terms democratic iterations. Exclusion is not solely a result of the denial of citizenship; citizens may also face various forms of exclusion from the political community through discriminatory practices that prevent a citizen's ability to participate in democratic deliberation or the decision-making process. For example, national and indigenous minorities who hold citizenship status may still suffer from constraints on their membership—when understood as *inclusion*—in the polity based on cultural and identity-based differences or the extent to which they challenge the democratic legitimacy of the existing state.

Rainer Bauböck,* a prominent scholar of migration and citizenship, is among Benhabib's critics who found her omission of this matter troubling. He argued that Benhabib failed to address "the rights of others within liberal democracies whose 'otherness' is not related to their foreign origin and citizenship but to their exclusion from a dominant nation-building project within the state."[10]

Although Benhabib made it clear in her text that she was concerned with the rights of immigrants, refugees, and asylum seekers looking for admittance into a state that was not their country of birth, what was neglected was any attention to the continuing challenges these people face, even after residence or citizenship rights have been awarded. A fuller account of how membership ought to be defined in the policies, practices, and institutions of democracies which endorse the inclusion of all members—including both citizens and aliens—of a polity may offer a more robust application of a right to membership than one that is exclusively concerned with the formal rules and procedures delineating naturalization and citizenship.

NOTES

1   Seyla Benhabib, *The Rights of Others: Aliens, Residents and Citizens, John Roberts Seeley Lectures* (Cambridge: Cambridge University Press, 2004), 171.

2   Benhabib, *The Rights of Others*, 73.

3   Michael Walzer, *Spheres of Justice: A Defense of Pluralism and Equality* (New York: Basic Books, 1983), 39.

4   United Nations General Assembly, *Universal Declaration of Human Rights*, December 10, 1948, 217 A, www.un.org/en/universal-declaration-human-rights/.

5   Benhabib, *The Rights of Others*, 11.

6   Seyla Benhabib, "The Morality of Migration," *The New York Times*, July 29, 2012, accessed March 1, 2018, https://opinionator.blogs.nytimes. com/2012/07/29/stone-immigration/.

7   Amy Allen, "The Rights of Others: Aliens, Residents and Citizens (Review)," *Hypatia* 22, no. 2 (2007): 200-204.

8   Seyla Benhabib, "Democratic Exclusions and Democratic Iterations: Dilemmas of "Just Membership" and Prospects of Cosmopolitan Federalism," *European Journal of Political Theory* vol. 6, no. 4 (2007): 453.

9   Seyla Benhabib, "Democratic Exclusion and Democratic Iterations," 453.

10 Rainer Bauböck, "The Rights of Others and the Boundaries of Democracy," *European Journal of Political Theory* 6 (2007): 403.

MODULE 7
ACHIEVEMENT

KEY POINTS

- *The Rights of Others* addresses migration, human rights, citizenship, multiculturalism, and state sovereignty in an age of globalization.

- Seyla Benhabib makes an original contribution to political philosophy debates on global justice and a practical contribution to the needs of migrants.

- One important limitation of the text is that it focuses entirely on Europe and the United States.

Assessing the Argument

The introduction to Seyla Benhabib's *The Rights of Others: Aliens, Residents and Citizens* includes a detailed chapter outline that serves as a useful road map to navigate the subsequent chapters. Benhabib is a clear writer, elaborating the main stages of her argument in detail and then offering a concise summary of her main points in the concluding remarks of each chapter. The initial stages of the book are dedicated to a critical engagement with the relevant philosophical texts and normative positions of Immanuel Kant, Hannah Arendt, John Rawls, and Michael Walzer.

After establishing the broad theoretical framework, the subsequent chapters on the transformation of citizenship in contemporary Europe serve as useful tools for both academics and students to fully understand the cornerstones of Benhabib's argument. These include the main principles of discourse theory, the concept of "democratic iterations," as well as the "paradox of

> ❝ Benhabib makes two foundational contributions in this book. One is to bring philosophical thinking to the question of immigration, most particularly the question of the incorporation of non-citizens in liberal democracies. The second is her notion of democratic iterations by which she means a complex process of public argument, deliberation and learning through which formal political change can take place. ❞
>
> Saskia Sassen, "Response to Benhabib"

democratic legitimacy."[1] Furthermore, the three empirical case studies offer easily accessible examples of jurisgenerative politics.

These include the "headscarf debate," or *l'affaire du foulard*,* in France; the case of a German-Afghani schoolteacher who was denied the right to teach with her head covered in Germany; and a debate on the voting rights of foreign residents in the province of Schleswig-Holstein* and the city-state of Hamburg.

While many previous scholars, such as Stephen Castles* and Andrew Geddes,* have provided great insight on transnational migrants, refugees, and asylum seekers, Benhabib offers a rare contribution to the subject matter from both a philosophical and methodological perspective. She makes this an explicit objective of her work: "For too long normative political theory and the political sociology of the modern state have gone their separate ways."[2] The attempt to remedy this divergence is a testament to the value of her interdisciplinary research and serves as a useful tool for both academics and practitioners interested in linking cosmopolitan and global justice debates with the real-world needs of immigrants and refugees.

Achievement in Context

The Rights of Others engages with a theoretical debate that continues to vex political theorists, politicians, and lawmakers around questions of how nation-states ought to incorporate others into their existing polities and what obligations they have to do so. The originality of Benhabib's normative contribution derives principally from her assertion of the right to membership as a human right. This book constitutes an original response to the contemporary challenges posed by global patterns of transnational migration, the nature of states' legal and moral obligations toward immigrants, and the rights of non-nationals to appeal for the right to membership and citizenship from the perspective of political philosophy.

The Rights of Others is both a result of, and response to, the transforming boundaries of the *demos*—meaning the citizens of a state who by virtue of their citizenship status are entitled to authorize the content of democratic law—that are spurred on by unprecedented levels of worldwide migration and the growing number of immigrants, refugees, and newcomers seeking entry into foreign states.[3] It is a product of the empirical and normative challenges facing contemporary democracies in terms of citizenship, the rights of immigrants and asylum seekers, the accommodation of difference in multicultural societies, and territorial sovereignty in an age of globalization.

Limitations

Benhabib defended the right of immigrants to permanent residence, equal protection and, eventually, to full citizenship in Western, democratic states. However, the author did not explore the challenges faced in other parts of the world where transnational migrations take place, and neglected to discuss the responsibility of other types of political regimes (i.e. non-democratic systems) towards foreigners.

Although Benhabib's broader philosophical questions concern the guiding normative principles of membership in a globalizing world, she restricts her philosophical exploration to liberal democracies and her empirical focus to contemporary Europe (in great detail) and the United States (in minor detail). Her discussion pays attention to the rights claims articulated of "nationals of European Union (EU) member states who may be long-term residents in EU countries other than those of their nationality; resident third-country nationals who are non-EU citizens; as well as refugees and asylum seekers aspiring to legalized long-term residency within the European Union."[4]

Essentially, the "paradox of legitimacy" that sets the stage for Benhabib's argument—the tension between a state's commitment to universal human rights principles and claims of self-determination and territorial sovereignty—concern a broader range of states than Benhabib explicitly acknowledged. Signatories of international human rights conventions that lie outside the Western world are also inherently implicated in the types of questions that interest Benhabib.

NOTES

1   Seyla Benhabib, *The Rights of Others: Aliens, Residents and Citizens, John Roberts Seeley Lectures* (Cambridge: Cambridge University Press, 2004), 2.

2   Benhabib, *The Rights of Others*, 143.

3   Benhabib, *The Rights of Others*, 5.

4   Benhabib, *The Rights of Others*, 147–67; Seyla Benhabib, "Democratic Exclusions and Democratic Iterations: Dilemmas of "Just Membership" and Prospects of Cosmopolitan Federalism," *European Journal of Political Theory* 6 (2007): 457.

MODULE 8
PLACE IN THE AUTHOR'S WORK

KEY POINTS

- *The Rights of Others* is a revised and expanded version of the John Seeley lectures Seyla Benhabib delivered at the University of Cambridge in 2002.

- The core themes of the book are present in Benhabib's previous work.

- Benhabib is an eminent political theorist and a key representative of the cosmopolitan school of thought.

Positioning

Seyla Benhabib's main concerns in *The Rights of Others: Aliens, Residents and Citizens* can be traced back in embryo to her doctoral thesis on G. W. F. Hegel's *Philosophy of Right*, which examined the tensions between freedom, universal rights, and political membership in sovereign states. However, her lectures and publications from the late-1990s onwards represent a far more mature scholar who seeks to redefine the terms of philosophical debate on these issues. For example, in an article titled "Citizens, Residents, and Aliens in a Changing World: Political Membership in the Global Era (1999)," she described sovereignty as "the right of a collectivity to define itself by asserting power over a bounded territory" and claimed that "declarations of sovereignty, more often than not, create distinctions between 'us' and 'them.'"[1] She later reformulated this concept in *The Rights of Others* as the "paradox of legitimacy" at the core of liberal democracies. Benhabib described this paradox as one where the "republican sovereign should undertake to bind its will by a series of pre-commitments to a set of formal and substantive norms, usually referred to as 'human rights.'"[2]

> ❝ Hegel is one of the first systematic thinkers in modernity who says, 'Look, we have three principles in the state. There is morality, there is legality, and then there is ethical life.' That's what I focused on, and it seems to be for the last thirty years, I have been circling around this question in one way or another. ❞
>
> Seyla Benhabib, "Philosophical Iterations, Cosmopolitanism, and the 'Right to Rights,' Conversation with Seyla Benhabib."

The Rights of Others is a revised and expanded version of a series of talks Benhabib delivered as part of the John Robert Seeley Lectures at the University of Cambridge between April 27 and May 2, 2002. These talks broadened, modified, and continued reflections she had presented as the Spinoza Chair at the University of Amsterdam in 2001 under the title *Transformations of Citizenship: Dilemmas of the Nation-State in the Era of Globalization*. This revision and expansion stemmed from her academic interaction with students and scholars in Amsterdam; at Yale Law's School's Legal Theory Colloquium in 2002, where she received feedback from scholars including Bruce Ackerman* and Judith Resnik;* and in discussions she had at the University of Toronto with Joseph Carens,* among others.

Parts of *The Rights of Others* had been published previously. Chapter 1 had appeared as "Of Guests, Aliens and Citizens: Rereading Kant's Cosmopolitan Right (2001)." Chapter 2 has been published, in part, as "Political Geographies in a Changing World: Arendtian Reflections (2002)." Finally, a portion of chapter 4 had been published in "Transformations of Citizenship: The Case of Contemporary Europe (2002)."

Integration

Political philosophy has been Benhabib's long-standing concern and interest. She applied her understanding of discourse ethics to gender and cultural difference in earlier works, most notably *Situating the Self: Gender, Community, and Postmodernism in Contemporary Ethics* (1992). Benhabib's concern with the rights of immigrants, refugees, and asylum seekers is most evident in her book *The Reluctant Modernism of Hannah Arendt*, published in 1996. Inspired by Arendt's conception of statelessness and the "right to have rights," Benhabib began to contemplate the irony that despite the rise of international human rights norms and instruments, such as the 1948 UN Declaration on Human Rights, the enforcement of such rights remains conditional upon the willingness of states to uphold their commitment to universal principles within their own national borders. As such, *The Rights of Others* is the product of a mature thinker who has been contemplating issues around the philosophy of rights and the needs of immigrants, refugees, and asylum seekers for much of her scholarly career.

An important shift in Benhabib's philosophical work came in the mid-1990s when she began to turn to empirical questions around multiculturalism, citizenship, and immigration within the European Union. This coincided with the Treaty of Maastricht* (1992) and the creation of European citizenship.* In particular, she began focusing on the ways in which rights for European Union (EU)* citizens and third-country nationals were developing at different levels of governance (i.e. at the state level, the sub-state level, and the EU level).

She attributed this institutionalist and empirical evolution in her research to an interest in addressing the contemporary challenges facing societies.[3] The preoccupation with us-versus-them demarcations from a moral point of view lies at the heart of Benhabib's critical focus on the rules of membership and the practices of inclusion and exclusion that take place in democratic states. The questions she raised in an earlier article where she asked, "What kinds of immigration, naturalization, and citizenship practices then would be compatible with the commitments of liberal democracies to human rights?"[4] carry forward in Benhabib's intellectual framework and are explicit in

The Rights of Others and her subsequent work, such as *Another Cosmopolitanism* (2006). The result has been Benhabib's articulation for the need to move towards decriminalization of border movements, the formulation of a universally anchored system of protections for refugees and asylum seekers, and the extension of municipal voting, and other rights, for long-term residents of the EU.

Significance

Benhabib is an eminent political theorist who represents a universalist moral standpoint and a vision of cosmopolitan politics. She follows the Kantian tradition in thinking of cosmopolitanism as "the emergence of norms that ought to govern relations among individuals in a global civil society."[5]

Well-known scholars, such as Joseph Carens and Will Kymlicka,* have praised Benhabib for renewing attention to the aspirations of cosmopolitan thought in political theory, particularly through the publication of *The Rights of Others.* Although the book is mainly a project in cosmopolitanism, given its subject matter it inevitably straddles multiple disciplines, engaging with contemporary political thought, democratic theory, multiculturalist studies, human rights and refugee issues, as well as globalization literature. The ideas contained in the text have therefore had an impact both within and outside Benhabib's main field of contemporary political theory.

Benhabib's ideas have been adapted and applied to a range of topics including European Union political integration, the Eurozone financial crisis,* and the challenges of multiculturalism in Germany. Scholars in other disciplines, such as Kymlicka who focuses on nationalism, multiculturalism, and citizenship, share Benhabib's concerns on how to achieve universal human rights for all persons; the moral, legal, and political obligations of states to protect the rights of others; and the democratic legitimacy of immigration and citizenship procedures adopted by states.[6]

NOTES

1   Seyla Benhabib, "Citizens, Residents, and Aliens in a Changing World: Political Membership in the Global Era." *Social Research* 66, no. 3 (1999): 710.

2   Seyla Benhabib, *The Rights of Others: Aliens, Residents and Citizens, John Roberts Seeley Lectures* (Cambridge: Cambridge University Press, 2004), 47.

3   Harry Kreisler, "Philosophical Iterations, Cosmopolitanism, and the 'Right to Rights,' Conversation with Seyla Benhabib," *Institute of International Studies, UC Berkeley*, March 18, 2004, accessed March 1, 2018, http://globetrotter.berkeley.edu/people4/Benhabib/benhabib-con2.html.

4   Seyla Benhabib, *Transformations of Citizenship: Dilemmas of the Nation-State in an Age of Globalization* (Amsterdam: Van Gorcum Ltd, 2001), 27.

5   Seyla Benhabib, *Another Cosmopolit*anism (Oxford: Oxford University Press, 2006), 20.

6   Will Kymlicka, "Liberal Nationalism and Cosmopolitan Justice: Comments on Benhabib," in *Another Cosmopolitanism* (Oxford: Oxford University Press, 2006), chapter 5.

SECTION 3
IMPACT

MODULE 9
THE FIRST RESPONSES

KEY POINTS

- *The Rights of Others* has been critiqued from a number of angles by prominent scholars.

- Benhabib has responded to most criticisms, which has enhanced the overall value of the text.

- There is no consensus view on how best to reconcile the tensions between human rights and state sovereignty.

Criticism

Seyla Benhabib's *The Rights of Others: Aliens, Residents and Citizens* has received its fair share of criticism. These critiques have dealt primarily with Benhabib's concepts of just membership and democratic iterations, and her binary portrayal of states and international human rights regimes.

For example, Alexander Aleinikoff* has argued that Benhabib's framework does not go far enough to resolve an inherent problem in applying discourse theory to the explication of political membership practices. Those persons who are most affected by exclusionary practices and norms are often left outside the moral conversation or "democratic iteration" that justifies the terms of their exclusion. They are unable to contest the denial of their membership rights because, by definition, they are excluded and denied a democratic voice. Benhabib identified this problem, but left it unresolved.[1] As Aleinikoff puts it, "To say that any resident migrant has the right to participate in the conversation is to assert as a postulate the very issue that is under discussion in the conversation—the right of membership."[2]

> ❝ One of my core hypotheses is that the foundational, albeit partial, changes we see in the current phase of globalization are partly instantiated and constituted through foundational changes inside the state apparatus. These changes result from active making by state entities, not just Benhabib's 'fraying' of the nation state. ❞
> Saskia Sassen, "Response to Benhabib"

Aleinikoff has also questioned how feasible it is to actually achieve Benhabib's vision of a right to membership, along with its corollary requirements of eventual naturalization and citizenship for immigrants, given the diverse constitutional and legislative arrangements enforced by various democracies. He has suggested that a pursuit of the rights of others may be better served by recognizing the human rights of all individuals in a polity—whether citizens or not—on the basis of their fundamental rights as persons, rather than through an assertion of a specific right to membership.[3]

Another critic, Saskia Sassen,* has been skeptical about Benhabib's depiction of the fraying of state sovereignty, which, in her view, over-emphasizes the impact of globalization on the deconstruction of the state while neglecting to consider the role of the state in actively contributing to the *making* of the global system as it stands today.[4] Sassen expresses this as follows: "Benhabib's understanding of the character of the relationship between nation states and universal principles such as the human rights regime is predicated on a binary whereby the national and the global are mutually exclusive ... My research of the last 15 years shows that such binary analytics keep us from adequately understanding the foundational transformation afoot today."[5]

The fact that *The Rights of Others* has sparked such debate from high-profile scholars is a testament to the importance of the subject matter at hand, but also to Benhabib's ability to formulate a thought provoking and urgent appeal for the recognition of the rights of all those who may be deemed others.

Responses

In response to various criticisms, Benhabib revisited and clarified some of the main ideas behind the conceptual framework that she develops in *The Rights of Others*. While acknowledging the views of critics such as Angelia K. Means,* Rainer Bauböck, Saskia Sassen, and Thomas Alexander Aleinikoff, she defended the utility and reasoning behind her key assertions.

A critical dialogue occurred primarily through two forums which enabled Benhabib to engage with her critics. The proceedings of a symposium held by the North American Society for Social Philosophy appeared in *Science, Technology, and Social Justice* (2007), and further debate took place in the pages of *The European Journal of Political Theory* (Fall 2007), which dedicated a special section to *The Rights of Others*. Most critics focused on various details or subordinate aspects of Benhabib's assertions while finding her overall conceptual scheme plausible. In *Another Cosmopolitanism* (2006), Benhabib also engaged with renowned scholars Jeremy Waldron,* Bonnie Honig,* and Will Kymlicka.

One area that Benhabib has sought to clarify in response to criticism is her arguably ambiguous definition of porous borders. Benhabib maintains that what she suggested in her book meets the *logic* of democratic representation and asserts that representation necessarily involves boundaries or demarcation of some sort, though she certainly does not reject the possibility that demarcation may someday transcend or dissolve national boundaries. Although "the demos, as the popular sovereign, must assert control over a specific territorial domain," it is still possible that it can engage in "reflexive acts of self-constitution" whereby the boundaries of the demos—meaning rules that govern inclusion and justifiable exclusion, or distinctions between citizens and aliens—can be renegotiated.[6] Benhabib wants to make it clear that she interprets democratic closure and the need for boundaries as necessary for the logic of representation, which requires the delineation of units of representation from one another.[7]

In response to objections that the notion of democratic iterations cannot possibly include all the participants who are affected by a certain decision in its deliberation, Benhabib explains that she differentiates between the circulation of normative issues versus decisional structures.[8] Even if immigrants, refugees, or non-nationals cannot be part of formal decision-making regarding naturalization or citizenship policies, they can still be part of the democratic conversation. Attempting to make a stronger case for how democratic iterations can incorporate and promote cosmopolitan norms within the boundaries of states—an area she does not adequately clarify in *The Rights of Others*—Benhabib has later argued that the force of iterations will compel positive law, that is laws that include those who have been traditionally excluded, such as undocumented immigrants.

Conflict and Consensus

Despite the carefully defended reasoning behind Benhabib's engagement with her critics, the emergence of a consensus view on such highly-contested issues as immigration, refugees, membership, and citizenship is unfortunately difficult to imagine, given the politicized nature of these issues in many countries. At present, for example, it has been impossible for European Union leaders to agree on a response to the Syrian Refugee Crisis.* They have been unable to reconcile states' concerns over security and identity with the humanitarian needs of refugees and asylum seekers. This is but one practical example of the seemingly unresolvable tensions that exist between transnational movement and sovereignty.

Benhabib asserted that nation-states have a right to impose reasonable legislative constraints on membership, including language competence, a demonstration of civic literacy, or residency requirements. What she found objectionable—from a moral point of view—was the absence of any procedure or possibility for foreigners and resident aliens to become citizens at all. She also objected to naturalization being denied or restricted on the basis of "the *kind*" of being someone is, based on one's "ascriptive and non-elective attributes such as race, gender, religion, ethnicity, language community or sexuality."[9] She made a strong case for why liberal democracies should not deny a person membership in perpetuity or render them a permanent alien. *The Rights of Others* continues to exercise significant influence today in cosmopolitan thought, citizenship theory, political philosophy, and other fields. The intellectual debate on how to concretely achieve a cosmopolitan global justice is far from over, but few would disagree that Benhabib raises the right kind of questions.

NOTES

1   Seyla Benhabib, *The Rights of Others: Aliens, Residents and Citizens, John Roberts Seeley Lectures* (Cambridge: Cambridge University Press, 2004), 15.

2   Alexander Aleinikoff, "Comments on the Rights of Others," *European Journal of Political Theory* 6 (2007): 427–8.

3   Aleinikoff, "Comments on the Rights of Others," 427–8.

4   Sassen, Saskia, "Response," *European Journal of Political Theory* vol. 6, no. 4 (2007): 434.

5   Sassen, "Response," 435.

6   Benhabib, *The Rights of Others*, 48.

7   Mariano Croce et al., "Toward a Converging Cosmopolitan Project?," January 28, 2010, accessed March 5, 2018, https://www.opendemocracy.net/mariano-croce-daniele-archibugi-seyla-benhabib/toward-converging-cosmopolitan-project.

8   Seyla Benhabib, "Democratic Exclusions and Democratic Iterations: Dilemmas of 'Just Membership' and Prospects of Cosmopolitan Federalism," *European Journal of Political Theory* 6 (2007): 452.

9   Seyla Benhabib, *The Rights of Others*, 138–9.

MODULE 10
THE EVOLVING DEBATE

KEY POINTS

* Democratic iterations, jurisgenerative politics, and cosmopolitan federalism have become key conceptual terms in political philosophy.

* Benhabib represents one important strand of cosmopolitan scholarship.

* Though it is difficult to identify disciples of Benhabib, her work is an important reference point for neo-Kantian* scholars.

Uses and Problems

The core ideas Seyla Benhabib articulated in *The Rights of Others: Aliens, Residents and Citizens* reinforced her broader conceptualization of cosmopolitan federalism. This was done namely by her call for a human right to just membership and the constitutive role played by processes of democratic iterations and jurisgenerative politics in liberal democracies. By succinctly presenting the critical principles and tools that undergird this progressive vision, Benhabib's text challenged existing ideas that are dominant in the discipline, such as the sanctity of state borders or redistributive schemes designed to create economic justice among peoples to alleviate immigration pressures. The evolutionary influence of *The Rights of Others* is most evident in its ideas on the limits of nation-state authority and effectiveness under the strains of globalization; the emergence of transnational configurations; and the possibility of context-transcending or universal forms of membership. Subsequent to this book, Benhabib's theoretical and political research has evolved to further develop the role of

> ❝ Universal cosmopolitanism currently faces two barriers to its success. The ... necessary boundedness of democratic authority, and ... the historically specific forms of national solidarity represented by the ethnos ... Benhabib regards the first of these barriers as intrinsic to the tension between law and ethics, and she argues that it cannot be escaped but only ameliorated ... ❞
>
> Robert Post, "Introduction," *Another Cosmopolitanism*

international law in a world of increasing global interdependence. This lead her to develop a model of "jurisgenerativity" that examines democratic sovereignty's compatibility with transnational legal norms. By "jurisgenerativity," she means that globalization is allowing for the creation of new spaces in liberal democracies in which there is deliberation, principles and norms are challenged, learning occurs, and new terms and rights emerge. She promoted this cosmopolitan perspective based on the 1948 Universal Declaration of Human Rights in her subsequent works, including *Dignity in Adversity: Human Rights in Troubled Times* (2011) and *Equality and Difference: Human Dignity and Popular Sovereignty in the Mirror of Political Modernity* (2013).

Schools of Thought

Cosmopolitan political theorists have responded in various ways to concerns for global justice. For example, notable thinkers like Thomas Pogge have focused on global institutional structures and the question of how much justice these institutions are able to deliver in terms of fundamental rights and duties. Others, like Brian Barry* and Charles Beitz, have approached the requirements for global justice from the standpoint of global institutional systems that can serve the needs of all persons. Martha Nussbaum* has tackled the issue through an emphasis on the role of education in fostering empathy towards the plight of those suffering beyond our own borders. Although cosmopolitan theorists are inspired by Benhabib's commitment to achieving a right to membership for immigrants, refugees, and asylum seekers, there are important variations in the cosmopolitan school.

However, democratic theorists—like James Fishkin* and David Held*—subscribing to a model of deliberative democracy, which was a prominent intellectual school in the field of democratic theory, have generally identified with Benhabib's ideas pertaining to universalist deliberative democracy. In broad terms, these theorists contend that in a democracy, political decisions should follow a process of deliberation among free and equal persons. Benhabib argued that the deliberative model can transcend the dichotomy between the liberal emphasis on individual rights and liberties and the democratic emphasis on collective formation and will-formation.[1]

Although a sharply discernible school of thought has not yet emerged exclusively around Benhabib's works, she played a prominent role in shaping and challenging the existing paradigms in theories and approaches on cosmopolitanism, democracy, and human rights. For example, she has been influential in articulating one particular variant of cosmopolitanism, identifying a specifically *political* vision of cosmopolitan politics. Several key propositions contained in the text, such as cosmopolitan federalism, porous borders, and a right to membership can be highlighted as significant contributions to contemporary debate.

In Current Scholarship

The Rights of Others is an influential text in cosmopolitanism literature and highlights an issue—the morally defensible boundaries of political membership—that has received little attention among global justice theorists. But cosmopolitanism is not without its critics. Cosmopolitans have been called "dead souls," or blamed for being out of touch with ordinary citizens and their fundamental concerns. Benhabib has defended the relevance of a cosmopolitan vision of global civil society despite the emergence in many parts of the world of nationalism, xenophobia, and ethnic, racial or cultural discrimination against the other. She emphasized a cosmopolitanism which actively relates itself to diversity and inequality, and that is rooted in the notion of persons as moral beings who are entitled to rights by virtue of being human.

It is difficult to pinpoint an identifiable cluster of Benhabib's intellectual disciplines, but her ideas have had an impact on the development of a political cosmopolitanism, in particular through her advocacy of porous borders and a cosmopolitan federalism. This sort of argument fits into the philosophical movement that is concerned with political and institutional arrangements at the global level, and which have recently gravitated around neo-Kantian theorists such as Jürgen Habermas, John Rawls, Thomas Pogge, and Charles Beitz.

Among the author's key ideas, the concept of democratic iterations, which builds on Benhabib's earlier contributions to discourse ethics, has arguably received the greatest level of scholarly scrutiny. Critics, like Wallace Garrett Brown,* have argued that Benhabib does not sufficiently explain why democratic iterations would necessarily lead a democratic polity to adopt universal ethical norms.[2] Skeptics, such as Alexander Aleinikoff, have asked whether an alternative scenario—where a polity approves exclusionary policies that defend closed borders and non-admittance of migrants—should be deemed legitimate if the requirements of iteration are met by a democratic majority.[3] Such debate has helped spur new ideas and possible solutions to long-standing challenges on migration and human rights. Benhabib has expanded and elaborated upon the central tenets of the arguments she makes in *The Rights of Others* in her subsequent book *Another Cosmopolitanism: Hospitality, Sovereignty, and Democratic Iterations* (2006). Here, Benhabib defends the utility of democratic iterations as a process of integrating universal cosmopolitan norms into democratic practice. This text provides critical responses from Bonnie Honig, Jeremy Waldron, and Will Kymlicka who challenge and attempt to modify Benhabib's conceptualization of democratic iterations.

NOTES

1   Seyla Benhabib, "Toward a Deliberative Model of Democratic Legitimacy," in *Democracy and Difference: Contesting the Boundaries of the Political*, ed. Seyla Benhabib (Princeton, N.J: Princeton University Press, 1996), 77.

2   Garrett Wallace Brown, "Moving from Cosmopolitan Legal Theory to Legal Practice: Models of Cosmopolitan Law," in *The Cosmopolitanism Reader*, eds. Garret Wallace Brown and David Held (Cambridge: Polity Press, 2010), 262.

3   Alexander Aleinikoff, "Comments on the Rights of Others," *European Journal of Political Theory* 6 (2007): 427–8.

IMPACT AND INFLUENCE TODAY

KEY POINTS

- *The Rights of Others* is a seminal text in the disciplines of political philosophy and migration and refugee studies.

- Seyla Benhabib's cosmopolitan perspective continues to challenge the "decline-of-citizenship" school of thought.

- Benhabib's work expresses great hope that universal human rights will ultimately win out over nationalism and xenophobia.

Position

Seyla Benhabib's *The Rights of Others: Aliens, Residents and Citizens* is the winner of the North American Society for Social Philosophy's 2004 Best Book award as well as co-winner of the 2005 Ralph Bunche Award from the American Political Science Association. It has retained its relevance as a seminal text of political theory as well as a noteworthy contribution to the fields of migration and refugee studies.

The book has sparked productive debate since its publication. Despite being subject to considerable criticism, its inherent value as a well-articulated and impassioned plea for better treatment of immigrants and the membership rights of others has hardly been diminished. The consensus view is that the most original aspect of Benhabib's text rests in her articulation of the notion of democratic iterations, or "complex processes of public argument, deliberation and exchange through which universalist rights claims and principles are contested and contextualized." The idea that the seemingly unresolvable tension between a liberal democracy's commitment to universal human rights principles and their self-determination to

> ❝ For centuries, we have articulated issues of morality and ethics within a language of universalism. We have asked what we owe our fellow human beings, not what we owe our fellow citizens. Exemplary is the 'universalist moral standpoint' adopted by 'the discourse theory of ethics,' of which Seyla Benhabib is such an eminent representative. ❞
>
> Robert Post, "Introduction," *Another Cosmopolitanism*

control the "quality and quantity of the movement of peoples across state borders" can be mitigated and negotiated through democratic iterations carried out by the polity is a novel one.[1]

The significance of Benhabib's contribution to contemporary debate rests with her theoretically substantiated plea for recognizing membership as a human right of all persons regardless of their nationality. For Benhabib, if a process of deliberation is not carried out by the most inclusive participation of all those whose interests are affected, then the iterative process is not fully democratic, fair, or legitimate. In *The Rights of Others*, Benhabib proposes a concrete agenda for action, calling on states to transform existing rules and practices that separate citizens from aliens in liberal democracies. She defends a right to membership not only in moral terms but also maintains that it has legal implications and that states should incorporate such a right into their constitutions through clear and transparent naturalization and citizenship provisions.

Interaction

The book continues to confront what Benhabib labels "the decline-of-citizenship" school. According to Benhabib, proponents of this perspective should consider the "waning of the nation-state, whether under the impact of economic globalization, the rise of international human rights norms, or the spread of attitudes of cosmopolitan detachment, as resulting in the devaluation of citizenship as institution and practice."[2] Benhabib takes Michael Walzer's claims from his book *Spheres of Justice* (1983) as representative of this perspective that defends the sovereign privilege of the democratic people alone to regulate the movement of migrants and refugees across its territorial borders. For Walzer, cosmopolitans err by failing to sympathize with the attachments individuals carry for their countries. According to Benhabib, Walzer is skeptical about universal human rights claims, much less a human right to membership.[3] Furthermore, "decline-of-citizenship" theorists argue that the institution of citizenship is in danger of losing its meaning unless it remains embedded within bounded communities. Focusing on the work of David Jacobson,* Benhabib confronts scholars, such as Walzer, who see immigration as devaluing citizenship by fraying the political integrity or cultural cohesion of society. Benhabib challenges them by distinguishing cultural integration, with which the decline-of-citizenship school is primarily concerned, from political integration. The latter refers to "those practices and rules, constitutional traditions and institutional habits that bring individuals together to form a functioning political community."[4] She attempts to show that in liberal democracies the porousness of borders does not constitute a threat to, but rather enriches, existing democratic diversity.

Benhabib's alternative account of a modified Kantian "cosmopolitan federalism," which she sees as addressing the tension between universal human rights claims and states' claims as self-determining sovereigns over their territorial borders, constitutes a philosophical argument that continues to influence emerging ideas and interpretations on the subject today.[5] "A democratic culture," according to Benhabib, "requires an appreciation for moments of historical dilemma."[6] The philosophical and real world challenges posed by *The Rights of Others* are in keeping with Benhabib's wider intellectual endeavor to confront the difficult circumstances facing society today.

The Continuing Debate

In *The Rights of Others*, Benhabib confronts mainly those theorists she classifies under the decline-of-citizenship school. In particular, she refutes the views of prominent political philosopher Michael Walzer. He has responded with skepticism to Benhabib's calls for porous borders, questioning whether what she means by this is essentially "not open."[7] If that is the case, then Benhabib contradicts herself by conceding that there is a need for some form of political organization to control the flow of immigrants into an existing polity, but this is the Walzerian position that she painstakingly refutes. For Walzer, Benhabib is unclear on where she draws the line on the morally defensible level of regulative authority held by the nation-state. He also criticizes her for presenting an exaggerated account of the decline or transformation of the state, pointing out that the nation-state remains a crucial instrument of democratic politics, unrivalled by any existing global institution.[8]

There are various strands of thought within contemporary cosmopolitanism and considerable variation among them on how to define global justice or the approaches, institutions, and priorities that would best advance the cosmopolitan vision. For example, Benhabib opposes the global justice schemes developed by theorists such as Thomas Pogge and Charles Beitz. She objects to the imposition of a global redistributive principle to create economic justice among peoples that does not also take into account democratic self-governance and issues of membership. But despite certain differences, most cosmopolitan theorists are motivated by a shared commitment to achieving the goals of cosmopolitan global justice and the principles of universal and equal worth of all individuals beyond the traditional nation-state system.[9]

NOTES

1 Seyla Benhabib, *The Rights of Others: Aliens, Residents and Citizens, John Roberts Seeley Lectures* (Cambridge: Cambridge University Press, 2004), 118.

2 Benhabib, *The Rights of Others*, 115–16.

3 Benhabib, *The Rights of Others*, 114–15.

4 Benhabib, *The Rights of Others*, 121.

5 Saskia Sassen, "Response," vol. 6, no. 4 (2007): 431-444.

6 Seyla Benhabib, "Taking Ideas Seriously," 27, no. 6 (December 2002/ January 2003).

7 Michael Walzer, "In Response: Support for Modesty and the Nation-State," 11/2 (2001): 28-31.

8 "In Response: Support for Modesty and the Nation-State," 11, no. 2 (Spring 2001), http://www.gwu.edu/~ccps/rcq/rcq_inresponse_walzer.html.

9 Garret Brown Wallace and David Held, "Editors' Introduction," , eds. Garrett Brown Wallace and David Held (Cambridge: Polity Press, 2010), 1-15.

MODULE 12
WHERE NEXT?

KEY POINTS

- *The Rights of Others* will likely remain an important point of reference for political theorists, cosmopolitans, and migration scholars.

- In the future, Seyla Benhabib may extend her research to cover other geographical areas beyond the European Union.

- Benhabib's scholarship mediates the tensions between universal human rights and state sovereignty, and emphasizes the human needs of migrants.

Potential

Seyla Benhabib's *The Rights of Others: Aliens, Residents and Citizens* is likely to remain an enduringly influential contribution to contemporary political theory and cosmopolitan thought. The fact that the main issues Benhabib grapples with—such as the cross-border movement of migrants, refugees and asylum seekers, political membership in liberal democracies, and changes to the practice and institution of citizenship—continue to be debated and contested is testament to the value of the types of questions she raises and her application of philosophical thinking to the subject of immigration. The rights of others in the context of immigration have been predominantly addressed from the standpoints of legislative reform and domestic/international law. In turning to the needs of immigrants, refugees, and asylum seekers from a cosmopolitan worldview, Benhabib makes a notable and ambitious contribution to the subject.

> ❝ The position which I have characterized as cosmopolitan federalism suggests that, between the norms of international law and the actions of individual democratic legislatures, multiple "iterations" are possible and desirable. ❞
>
> Seyla Benhabib, *The Rights of Others*

The development of new approaches and ideas for the fulfillment of the rights of others in an era of fast-paced globalization are both necessary and inevitable. Benhabib's cosmopolitanism is not the only possibility for what the future of cosmopolitan politics may look like, but it presents a set of thought-provoking ideas that are ripe for debate and reconsideration.[1] A prolific author, Benhabib continues to write and speak extensively to elaborate and develop upon her earlier ideas.

Beyond raising important philosophical concerns, the book also has policy implications for immigration and naturalization legislation. Contemporary debates around the rights of undocumented immigrants in the United States or the legal and moral obligations of European Union member states towards refugees trying to escape poverty, civil war, or persecution in their home countries are examples of how Benhabib's concerns are relevant to the real world.

Future Directions

Looking ahead, it may be possible that Benhabib moves beyond her focus on the citizenship rights regimes of European Union member states to offer a more diversified set of cases drawn from other geographical regions or types of governments beyond the democracies of continental Europe. Since *The Rights of Others*, her analytical focus has evolved to attribute a greater role to legal institutions and international/domestic law in fostering cosmopolitan ideals in practice, largely through the application of her innovative concept of democratic iterations. Given Benhabib's important contributions to feminist theory, it may be expected that she looks in greater depth at the gendered dimensions of transnational migrations in future publications.

The main ideas contained in *The Rights of Others* have been debated since its publication by scholars in the fields of law, political theory, multicultural studies, and human rights, among others. As Benhabib puts it, whether the transnational movement of peoples is caused by economic migrants from the poorer regions of the world seeking new opportunities in resource-rich democracies in the north and the west, or "whether they are undertaken by asylum and refuge seekers escaping persecution, civil wars and natural disasters" such movements pose unprecedented challenges across the globe.[2] Benhabib's book underlines how urgent it is that theorists engage with the real-world dilemmas affecting people's lives, such as existing practices of exclusion. Benhabib seeks to move beyond a moral critique to an actual road map for democratic politics. Given that the solution to these challenges remains elusive, the moral, legal, and political relevance of the book remains significant for the foreseeable future.

Summary

The ideas expressed in *The Rights of Others* reflect the importance and challenges of the transnational movement of people. Although migration is not a new issue, what is a recent phenomenon is the rise of universal human rights principles which undermine state sovereignty. The cross-border movements of peoples, and particularly those of refugees and asylum seekers, are now subject to a robust international human rights regime. At the same time, in spite of international treaties that stipulate the rights of all by virtue of their common humanity rather than citizenship, state policies still largely regulate who enters their territories. Border fences and controls, interceptions at sea, detentions, and the refusal to grant asylum are but a few examples of the realities often faced by others in their pursuit of a better life.

The Rights of Others bridges a gap between the normative-analytical discourse at the heart of political theory and the needs of migrants and refugees. The concern is not to appeal to adherents of a particular scholarly discipline, but rather to widen the parameters of the debate to highlight the relevance of the issue of membership rights to multiple and interrelated disciplines. Benhabib aims to reach an interdisciplinary audience by encouraging political philosophy to become better attuned to sociological trends and put identifiable human stakes into debates over territoriality, democratic voice, and citizenship. Following from this objective, the text targets a diverse range of scholars rooted in political and legal philosophy, social theory and multicultural scholarship, refugee and migration studies, and human rights. Benhabib's aspiration to reconcile the competing demands of universalism and particularism inherent to discussions around human rights has sparked considerable debate both within and outside the book's immediate purview of cosmopolitan political theory.

The Rights of Others was a timely and not merely theoretical response to the challenges faced by democracies as they evaluate demands for broader membership rights for non-citizens, given the obligations imposed upon states by the international human rights regime and evolution of legal norms. Under such circumstances, most democracies face pressure from domestic and global civil society, immigration and human rights activists, citizens, residents, and aliens to formulate immigration policies and national asylum management systems that align with their commitment to universal human rights principles. Benhabib responds to such pressing challenges by proposing a model for membership rights that is more democratically inclusive, while still acknowledging the rights of states to defend their national borders.

NOTES

1   Saskia Sassen, "Response," *European Journal of Political Theory*, vol. 6, no. 4 (2007): 431-444.

2   Seyla Benhabib, "Democratic Exclusions and Democratic Iterations: Dilemmas of "Just Membership" and Prospects of Cosmopolitan Federalism," *European Journal of Political Theory* vol. 6, no. 4 (2007): 445.

GLOSSARY

GLOSSARY OF TERMS

Active citizenship: in addition to having rights, members of a community have responsibilities towards the common good, such as voting, volunteering, recycling, and running for public office.

Alien: in legal terms, an alien is a person who is not a citizen of the country in which she or he resides.

Antiquity: the ancient past, especially the period of classical and other human civilizations before the Middle Ages (OED).

Asylum seeker: a person who is seeking protection as a refugee and is still waiting to have his/her claim assessed.

Capitalism: an economic system that emphasizes the private ownership of the means of production. The means of production refers to those things that are necessary for the production of goods, such as land, natural resources, and technology.

Christianity: religion based on the person and teachings of Jesus Christ, or its beliefs and practices (OED).

Civic culture: a term coined by Almond and Verba (1963) and further developed by Inglehart (1988, 1990) that refers to how attitudes shape democracy. By attitudes, they mean trust between citizens, confidence in the political system, and a belief in one's ability to influence politics and society.

Classical liberalism: a political ideology that developed in the early nineteenth century and advocated individual liberties, free market economics, and the pursuit of private property. It was based on the ideas of Adam Smith, John Locke, and others.

Communicative rationality: Jürgen Habermas distinguishes between two types of rationality, communicative action and strategic action. The former is aimed at conflict resolution through compromise; the latter is based on the calculative manipulation of others.

Cosmopolitan federalism: Seyla Benhabib's vision of cosmopolitan federalism acknowledges the enduring significance of a person's membership within a bounded community, while also recognizing the need for other forms of "democratic attachment"—for example at the subnational or supranational levels—that may go beyond existing state structures. Cosmopolitan federalism makes it possible to negotiate "between the norms of international law and the actions of individual democratic legislatures" through the use of what Benhabib calls "democratic iterations."

Cosmopolitanism: a complex school of thought, cosmopolitanism's ethical orientation essentially maintains that there are moral obligations owed to all human beings based solely on our humanity. Cosmopolitanism is universal in its scope, holding that the moral standing of all humans applies to everyone equally and assumes that we are all citizens of the world.

1948 Declaration of Human Rights: adopted by the General Assembly of the United Nations in Paris after World War II, this declaration is a common standard for the universal protection of human rights for all peoples of all nations.

Decline-of-citizenship school: Benhabib uses this term to refer to political theorists who claim that globalization, migrants, and refugees are weakening the fabric of nations and their citizenship regimes.

Deliberative democracy: a political philosophy that asserts that political decisions in democracies should result from a fair and reasoned discussion between citizens.

Democratic iterations: a term used by Seyla Benhabib to refer to "complex processes of public argument, deliberation and exchange through which universalist rights claims are contested and contextualized, invoked and revoked, posited and positioned throughout legal and political institutions as well as in the associations of civil society."

Demos: Seyla Benhabib uses the Greek term *demos* to describe the citizens of a state who by virtue of their citizenship status are entitled to authorize the content of democratic law. She compares this to the situation of legal or illegal aliens who are subject to the jurisdiction of state law but cannot take part in the decision-making process.

Denationalization/denaturalization: to deprive one of nationality and citizenship rights. Seyla Benhabib uses this term primarily in relation to Jews who lost their rights in different historical contexts, including fifteenth century Spain and Nazi Germany.

De-territorialized citizenship: Seyla Benhabib describes this as follows: "political identity need not be conceived in territorial terms: the boundaries of the civic community and the boundaries of the national territory need not be coextensive."

Discourse ethics: only those norms and normative institutional arrangements are valid which can be agreed to by all concerned under special argumentation situations named discourses.

Due process: receiving fair treatment under the judicial system.

Economic globalization: a term that describes the free movement of goods, capital, services, technology, and information. It also entails the increasing economic integration and interdependence among people and countries.

Enlightenment: an intellectual movement from the mid-seventeenth through the eighteenth century that was pioneered by European intelligentsia ushering in new ideas on progress, freedom, and human reason that parted from the medieval worldview based on dogmatic beliefs and religious doctrine.

Ernest Block Prize: a prestigious prize given every three years in Germany to distinguished philosophers.

European Union: a union of 28 countries established by the Treaty of the European Union (1993) that replaced the European Community, which had been founded in 1958 by the Treaty of Rome.

European Union citizenship: all citizens of European Union (EU) member states are EU citizens. The Treaty of Maastricht (1992) created this as an extension of national citizenship. It allows those citizens to reside and work in other member states, in addition to other benefits.

Eurozone financial crisis: linked to the Global Financial Crisis, since 2009, the Eurozone has been characterized by bank bailouts, debt crises, austerity, and high youth unemployment.

Frankfurt School: a philosophical and sociological movement that was originally associated with the Institute for Social Research at Goethe University in Frankfurt. It refers to a group of prominent scholars including Max Horkheimer and Theodor Adorno who popularized the dialectical method of learning.

Geneva Conventions of 1949 (and their additional protocols): the most important international treaties detailing humanitarian law and regulating armed conflict.

German idealism: a philosophical movement associated with Romanticism and the Enlightenment that started in Germany in the late eighteenth century as a reaction to the work of Immanuel Kant.

Global justice: an area of political philosophy that addresses the relationship between human beings, fairness, and equality. The works of scholars such as John Rawls and Seyla Benhabib deal extensively with this theme.

Globalization: the process whereby the world becomes more interconnected. Such interconnectedness takes many forms including economic, political, and cultural.

Headscarf Debate/*L'Affaire du Foulard*: a controversy that arose in France in 1989 after three students were suspended from Gabriel Havez Middle School in Creil for allegedly violating the principle of *laïcité* (secularity) by refusing to remove their Islamic headscarves. Variants of this debate remain active in France today.

Imperialism: the extension of a nation's influence by territorial acquisition or by the establishment of political and economic dominance over other nations.

Iterative acts: Seyla Benhabib describes these as "processes whereby cosmopolitan norms and the will of democratic majorities can be reconciled, though never perfectly, through public argumentation and deliberation."

Just membership: a term used by Seyla Benhabib in her defense of the right of all migrants and asylum seekers to legal citizenship in their host countries. However, she argues that states should be able to determine the path or conditions for full membership, as long as they always respect international human rights norms.

Ladino: Romance language derived from Old Spanish and Hebrew used by Sephardic Jews.

Leopold Lucas award: a prize awarded annually for outstanding work in the fields of theology, the history of ideas, history, and philosophy.

Liberal democracy: a political system that emphasizes human and civil rights, regular and free elections between competing political parties, and adherence to the rule of law.

Meister Eckhart Prize: a biannual prize given to scholars who produce important work on the subject of identity.

Multiculturalism: a political philosophy that rejects the idea that minority groups should assimilate into the dominant culture. Rather, it promotes the idea that minority groups can maintain their distinctive collective identities and practices.

Nation-state: a state that, in theory, is comprised predominantly of a common culture, history, and language.

Nationalism: the devotion to the interests of a particular nation-state.

Natural rights: those rights to which all human beings are entitled by virtue of their existence.

Naturalization: the process by which a non-national becomes a citizen of a country.

Neo-Kantian: those scholars who have revived the ideas of Immanuel Kant.

Normative a philosophical term to describe statements that are based on values. A normative statement is a claim about how things *should* or *ought* to be.

Open borders: Joseph Carens is the most well-known advocate of open borders. He argues that the free movement of people across borders should be a universal human right. However, his philosophy does allow for minor exceptions: for example, states could refuse entry to those deemed a threat to public security, such as terrorists.

Other: a term widely used in the social sciences to denote persons or groups who are generally viewed as different from the culture, ethnicity, language, or ideology of the majority in any given society.

Ottoman Empire: from the conquest of the Byzantine capital city of Constantinople in 1453 until its demise in World War I, the Ottoman Empire was an important global power. At the height of its power in the sixteenth and seventeenth centuries, particularly under the reign of Suleiman the Magnificent, the empire stretched from Hungary to Yemen, from Algiers to the Crimea and Iraq, controlling much of southeast Europe, Western Asia and North Africa. The Ottomans ruled over a rich multiplicity of peoples who followed different religions and spoke Turkic, Greek, Slavic, Albanian, Arabic, and Hungarian.

Particularistic: a term used to refer to groups that consider themselves to be special or unique due to class, race, religion, ethnicity, etc. This concept entails a mentality of closure towards those perceived to be outside their group.

***Philosophy of Right*:** a book published by Georg Wilhelm Friedrich Hegel in 1821 that details his legal, moral, social, and political philosophy.

Pluralism: this refers to a political system in which power is distributed among multiple groups.

***Polis*:** taken literally, the classical definition of the Greek term *polis* refers to a city-state in Ancient Greece. The usage in this text promotes a deliberative identification with a single cosmopolitan community, subscribed to on the basis of our shared humanity.

Political membership: Seyla Benhabib argues that all migrants and refugees should have access to full political membership or legal citizenship in their host countries.

Polity: a specific form of political organization or the condition of being constituted as a state or other organized community.

Porous borders: Seyla Benhabib asserts that no human is illegal, therefore everyone should have a path to full membership. However, she does not advocate borders, instead claiming that states should have the sovereignty to dictate the conditions necessary for migrants and asylum seekers to obtain legal citizenship.

Post-national: the process by which nation-states and national identities partially or entirely lose their importance due to supranational or global phenomena.

Ralph Bunche Prize: an award given annually by the American Political Science Association for the most important scholarly work in political science that addresses ethnic and cultural pluralism.

Reconquest (or *Reconquista*): military battles by which Christians reclaimed control of the Iberian Peninsula from the Moors, from roughly 711 to 1492.

Redistributive justice: a concept in political philosophy promoted by John Rawls and other scholars that asserts that developed countries should take measures to ensure a redistribution of resources to lesser developed countries in order to lessen inequalities and achieve greater global justice.

Refugee: the 1951 Convention Relating to the Status of Refugees (and its 1967 Protocol), defines a refugee as: "Any person who owing to a well-founded fear of being persecuted for reasons of race, religion, nationality, membership of a particular social group or political opinion, is outside the country of his/her nationality and is unable or, owing to such fear, is unwilling to avail himself/herself of the protection of that country."

Schleswig-Holstein: Germany's northernmost state.

Self-determination: the process by which a country determines its own statehood and forms its own government (OED).

Sephardic Jews: those who descend from Jews who lived in the Iberian Peninsula in the late fifteenth century, prior to the Alhambra Decree of 1492.

Sovereignty (or state sovereignty): supreme power of a state to govern its territory and polity without foreign interference.

Spanish Inquisition: a process of interrogation, investigation, and punishment carried out by the Catholic Church in Spain starting in the fifteenth century against converted Jews and Muslims alleged to be insincere.

State-centric international system: a system in which states are the most important actors in International Relations, and they exercise sovereignty over their borders. This is considered essential for power and security.

Statelessness: the UN describes statelessness as "a person who is not considered as a national by any state under the operation of its law." In other words, someone who is stateless does not have a nationality of any country.

Subnational: of, relation to, or designating a region or group within a nation (OED).

Supranational: having power or influence that transcends national boundaries or governments (OED). The European Union is sometimes referred to as a supranational body.

Syrian Refugee Crisis: since the Syrian Civil War started in 2011, according to the UN, more than 6 million Syrians have become internally displaced, and about 5 million refugees have fled Syria.

Third country nationals: this term is normally used within the European Union to refer to those residents who are from countries outside of the 28 member states.

Treaty of Maastricht: established in 1992, it created the European Union (replacing the European Community) and European citizenship, and stipulated the creation of the Common Monetary Policy.

Universal human rights: those rights to which all human beings are entitled by virtue of their existence. The 1948 Declaration of Human Rights describes these in detail.

Vietnam War: A military conflict (1955-1975) between South Vietnam, supported by the United States, and Communist North Vietnam. Du Bois's communist vision of society in the late stage of his life was shaped by Cold War events, including the Vietnam War.

World citizenship: the cosmopolitan idea that a global identify can supersede local, regional, and national identities based on a common commitment to humanity.

PEOPLE MENTIONED IN THE TEXT

Bruce Ackerman (b. 1943) is Sterling Professor at Yale Law School and the author of *Social Justice in the Liberal State*. Seyla Benhabib acknowledges Ackerman as one of the scholars at Yale Law's School's Legal Theory Colloquium in 2002 who helped her revise and expand her John Seeley lectures into *The Rights of Others*.

Thomas Alexander Aleinikoff (b. 1952) is Professor of Law at Georgetown University and the former Executive Associate Commissioner for Programs in the US Department of Justice's Immigration and Naturalization. He has published numerous articles in the areas of immigration, refugee and citizenship law and policy, and is the author of the critique: "Comments on the Rights of Others."

Hannah Arendt (1906–75) was one of the most influential political philosophers of the twentieth century. She is best known for two works that had a major impact both within and outside the academic community: *The Origins of Totalitarianism* (1951) and *The Human Condition* (1958). Her concept "the right to have rights" was one of the foundations for Seyla Benhabib's *The Rights of Others*.

Aristotle (384–322 B.C.E.) was an ancient Greek philosopher, and one of the most renowned thinkers of all time. Aristotle's *Politics* and *Nicomachean Ethics* influenced Seyla Benhabib's understanding of deliberative democracy in *The Rights of Others*.

Brian Barry (1936–2009) was Lieber Professor Emeritus of Political Science at Columbia University and Professor Emeritus of Political Science at the London School of Economics. He wrote several important works on social justice, including *Why Social Justice Matters*, *The Liberal Theory of Justice*, and *Liberty and Justice: Essays in Political Theory*.

Rainer Bauböck (b. 1953) is Professor of Social and Political Theory and from 2012 is Dean of Graduate Studies at the European University Institute. His research interests include normative political theory and comparative research on democratic citizenship, European integration, migration, nationalism, and minority rights.

Charles Beitz (b. 1949) is Professor of Politics and Director of the University Center for Human Values at Princeton University. His philosophical and teaching interests focus on contemporary political philosophy, international political theory, democratic theory, the theory of human rights, and the theory of property rights.

Wallace Garrett Brown is Chair in Political Theory and Global Health Policy at the University of Leeds. His work deals with Kant's political and legal theory, cosmopolitanism, deliberative theory, the laws of hospitality, and global justice.

Joseph Carens (b. 1945) is Professor of Political Science at the University of Toronto. His research deals with political theory, ethics, migration, and citizenship, and he is one of the leading advocates of open borders.

Stephen Castles (b. 1944) retired from his position in 2016 as Research Chair in Sociology at the University of Sydney. He is one of the foremost scholars of migration studies and the author of *Migration, Citizenship, and Identity* (2017), among other important works.

Robert Cover (1943–86) was a professor at Yale Law School from 1972 until his death in 1986. His most noted works include *Justice Accused: Antislavery and the Judicial Process, Violence and the Word*, and *Nomos and Narrative*.

Jacques Derrida (1930–2004) was a notable Algerian-born French philosopher and is considered to be one of the most influential thinkers of the twentieth century. He is the founder of deconstruction, a way of criticizing not only literary and philosophical texts but also political institutions. His work on language and iterations helped shape Seyla Benhabib's understanding of deliberative democracy in *The Rights of Others*.

James Fishkin (b. 1948) is Janet M. Peck Chair in International Communication at Stanford University and the director of Stanford's Center for Deliberative Democracy. He is the author of several important works, including *Democracy and Deliberation* and *The Dialogue of Justice*.

Andrew Geddes (b. 1965) is Director of the Migration Policy Centre and Chair in Migration Studies at European University Institute. He is the author of *The Politics of Migration and Immigration in Europe* (2003), among many other important works.

Jürgen Habermas (b. 1929) is considered one of the most influential philosophers in the world. His extensive written work addresses topics ranging from social-political theory to aesthetics, epistemology, and language to the philosophy of religion. His ideas have significantly impacted the evolution of philosophical debate as well as political-legal thought, sociology, communication studies, argumentation theory and rhetoric, developmental psychology, and theology.

Georg Wilhelm Friedrich Hegel (1770–1831) belongs to the period of German idealism, which developed towards the end of the eighteenth century primarily as a reaction against the philosophy of Kant. His views on morality, ethics, history, society, and the state are seen to be among his most enduring influence.

David Held (b. 1951) is Professor of Politics and International Relations at Durham University. He is the author of *Cosmopolitanism: Ideals and Realities* (2010), among other important works.

Thomas Hobbes (1588–1679) was an English political philosopher, best known today for his political commentary *Leviathan*. Hobbes's work is considered one of the foundations for political philosophy and European liberal thought.

Bonnie Honig (b. 1959) is Nancy Duke Lewis Professor-Elect of Modern Culture and Media and Political Science at Brown University. She is the author of *Feminist Interpretations of Hannah Arendt* (1995) and *Democracy and the Foreigner* (2003), among other important works.

David Jacobson is a political sociologist interested in the areas of immigration and citizenship, international institutions and law, human rights, religion and conflict, and women's status in global conflict. He is the founding director of the Citizenship Initiative, and Professor of Sociology at the University of South Florida.

Immanuel Kant (1724–1804), born in Königsberg, the capital of East Prussia (today Kaliningrad, Russia), is one of the most influential philosophers in the history of Western philosophy and is known as the paradigmatic philosopher of the European Enlightenment. He is the author of *Critique of Pure Reason* and *Perpetual Peace*, the latter of which is considered the modern foundation of liberalist theory in International Relations and cosmopolitanism.

Will Kymlicka (b. 1962) is the Canada Research Chair in Political Philosophy at Queen's University, where he has taught since 1998. His research interests focus on issues of democracy and diversity, and in particular on models of citizenship and social justice within multicultural societies.

Emmanuel Levinas (1906–1995) was a French philosopher known for his critique of ontology. His most important works are *De l'existence à l'existant* (*Existence and Existents*), *En découvrant l'existence avec Husserl et Heidegger* (*Discovering Existence with Husserl and Heidegger*), and *Autrement qu'être; ou, au-delà de l'essence* (*Otherwise than Being; or, Beyond Essence*).

John Locke (1632–1704) was an English philosopher, the father of classical liberalism, and one of the most influential thinkers of the Enlightenment movement. His most influential work is *Two Treatises on Government*.

Angelia K. Means is a scholar whose research interests include political recognition and justice; transmigration and communication; and nations, borders, and democracy. She is assistant professor in the Department of Government at Dartmouth College.

Martha Nussbaum (b. 1947) is an American philosopher and political theorist, known for her work expanding theories of justice to account for the conditions of women and the economically disadvantaged. Her *Frontiers of Justice: Disability, Nationality, Species Membership* elaborated her theory of human capabilities as an addendum to John Rawls's theory of justice.

Hanna Pitkin (b. 1931) is a Professor Emerita of Political Science at the University of California, Berkeley. She is a political theorist whose diverse interests range from the history of European political thought from ancient to modern times, through ordinary language philosophy and textual analysis, to issues of psychoanalysis and gender in political and social theory.

Plato (fourth century B.C.E.) was an ancient Greek philosopher. Founder of the Academy in Athens, the first university in the Western world, Plato, along with his teacher Socrates and his student Aristotle, laid the foundations of philosophy and science.

Thomas Pogge (b. 1953) is the Director of the Global Justice Program and the Leitner Professor of Philosophy and International Affairs at Yale University. Pogge has published widely on Kant and in moral and political philosophy, including various books on Rawls and global justice.

John Rawls (1921–2002) was an American political philosopher whose theory of "justice as fairness" envisions a society of free citizens holding equal basic rights cooperating within an egalitarian economic system. Rawls first set out justice as fairness in systematic detail in his 1971 book, *A Theory of Justice*; he continued to rework justice as fairness throughout his life, restating the theory in *Political Liberalism* (1993), *The Law of Peoples* (1999), and *Justice as Fairness* (2001).

Judith Resnik is the Arthur Liman Professor of Law at Yale Law School. Her work deals with justice, migration, and citizenship, and she co-edited the book *Migration and Mobilities: Citizenship, Borders, and Gender* with Seyla Benhabib.

Jean-Jacques Rousseau (1712–78) was a Genevan political philosopher who greatly influenced the French Revolution. Among his great works are *On the Social Contract* and *Discourse on the Origin and Basis of Inequality Among Men*.

Edward Saïd (1935–2003) was a Palestinian–American post-colonial literary theorist and university professor at Columbia University. He was one of the pioneers of post-colonial scholarship and the author of *Orientalism* (1978).

Judith N. Shklar (1928–92) was a political philosopher and John Cowles Professor of Government at Harvard University. She authored a number of books, including *Men and Citizens* and *Freedom and Independence*.

Saskia Sassen (b. 1947) is Professor of Sociology at Columbia University and Co-Chair of The Committee on Global Thought. Her research and writing focuses on globalization, immigration, global cities, new networked technologies, and changes within the liberal state that result from current transnational conditions.

Jeremy Waldron (b. 1953) is a professor of legal and political philosophy at NYU School of Law. He is the author of *Toleration and its Limits* (2008) and *One Another's Equals: The Basis of Human Equality* (2017), among other important works.

Michael Walzer (born 1935) is Professor Emeritus at the Institute for Advanced Study. He is one of America's foremost political thinkers and has written about a wide variety of topics in political theory and moral philosophy, including political obligation, just and unjust war, nationalism and ethnicity, economic justice, and the welfare state.

Max Weber (1864–1920) is widely regarded as one of the founders of the field of sociology. He also made important contributions to other fields, including political science, history, and economics. One of Seyla Benhabib's primary research areas is Weber's work.

WORKS CITED

WORKS CITED

Ágoston, Gábor, and Bruce Masters. *Encyclopedia of the Ottoman Empire*. New York Facts On File, 2009.

Aleinikoff, Alexander T. "Comments on the Rights of Others," *European Journal of Political Theory* 6, no.4 (2007).

Allen, Amy. "The Rights of Others: Aliens, Residents and Citizens (Review)." *Hypatia* 22, no. 2 (2007): 200–4.

Arendt, Hannah. *The Origins of Totalitarianism*. New York: Harcourt, Brace and Jovanovich, [1951] 1968.

Bauböck, Rainer. "The Rights of Others and the Boundaries of Democracy." *European Journal of Political Theory* 6, no. 4(2007).

Benhabib, Seyla. *Another Cosmopolitanism*. Oxford; New York: Oxford University Press, 2006.

– "Citizens, Residents, and Aliens in a Changing World: Political Membership in the Global Era." *Social Research* 66, no. 3 (1999): 36.

– *The Claims of Culture: Equality and Diversity in the Global Era*. Princeton, N.J.; Oxford: Princeton University Press, 2002.

– ed. *Democracy and Difference: Contesting the Boundaries of the Political*. Princeton, N.J.; Chichester: Princeton University Press, 1996.

– "Democratic Exclusions and Democratic Iterations: Dilemmas of "Just Membership" and Prospects of Cosmopolitan Federalism." *European Journal of Political Theory* 6, no 4. (2007).

– "The Morality of Migration." *The New York Times* (July 29 2012).

– "Reclaiming Universalism: Negotiating Republican Self-Determination and Cosmopolitan Norms." Paper presented at The Tanner Lectures on Human Values, March 15–19 2004.

– *The Rights of Others: Aliens, Residents and Citizens*. John Roberts Seeley Lectures. Cambridge: Cambridge University Press, 2004.

– "Taking Ideas Seriously." *Boston Review* 27, no. 6 (December 2002/January 2003).

– *Transformations of Citizenship: Dilemmas of the Nation-State in an Age of Globalization*. Amsterdam: Van Gorcum Ltd, 2001.

Bohman, James, and William Rehg. "Jürgen Habermas." In *The Stanford Encyclopedia of Philosophy,* edited by Edward N. Zalta. http://plato.stanford. edu/archives/win2011/entries/habermas/.

Brown, Garrett Wallace, and David Held, eds. *The Cosmopolitanism Reader.* Cambridge: Polity Press, 2010.

Calhoun, Craig, ed. *Habermas and the Public Sphere.* Cambridge MA: MIT Press, 1992.

d'Entreves, Maurizio Passerin. "Hannah Arendt." In *The Stanford Encyclopedia of Philosophy,* edited by Edward N. Zalta. http://plato.stanford.edu/archives/ fall2008/entries/arendt/.

Eriksens, Erik O. "Challenges to Cosmopolitanism in Contemporary Europe." Paper presented at the ARENA Centre for European Studies, 2012.

Habermas, Jurgen. *Moral Consciousness and Communicative Action.* Cambridge, MA.: MIT Press, [1983] 1990.

Hobsbawm, Eric. "The Future of the State." *Development and Change* 27, no. 2 (1996): 267–78.

Horstmann, Rolf-Peter. "Hegel, Georg Wilhelm Friedrich." In *Routledge Encyclopedia of Philosophy*, edited by Edward Craig. London: Routledge, (1998, 2004). http://www.rep.routledge.com/article/DC036.

Jacobson, David. *Rights across Borders: Immigration and the Decline of Citizenship.* Baltimore and London: Johns Hopkins University Press, 1997.

Kant, Immanuel. "Perpetual Peace." In *On History*, edited by Lewis White Beck. Indianapolis and New York: Library of Liberal Arts, [1795] 1957.

Kreisler, Harry, Interview with. "Philosophic Iterations, Cosmopolitans, and the "Right to Rights."" (March 18 2004).

Means, Angelia. "The Rights of Others." *European Journal of Political Theory* 6, no.4 (2007).

Orend, Brian. *War and International Justice: A Kantian Perspective.* Ontario, Canada: Wilfrid Laurier University Press, 2000.

Osborn, Ronald. "Seyla Benhabib, Wendell Berry, and the Question of Migrant and Refugee Rights." *Humanitas (National Humanities Institute)* 23, no. 1 (2010).

Said, Edward. *Orientalism*. New York: Pantheon, 1978.

Sandel, Michael. *Democracy's Discontent: America in Search of a Public Philosophy.* Cambridge, MA.: Belknap Press at Harvard University, 1996.

Sassen, Saskia. "Response." *European Journal of Political Theory* 6, no. 4

(2007).

United Nations General Assembly, *Universal Declaration of Human Rights*, December 10, 1948, 217 A, www.un.org/en/universal-declaration-human-rights/.

Urbinati, Nadia. "The Politics of Immigration and Membership." *Dissent* 52, no. 4 (2005).

Utlu, Deniz. "Interview with Seyla Benhabib: The Guest Is Always a Fellow Citizen." (October 26 2009). http://en.qantara.de/The-Guest-is-Always-a-Fellow-Citizen/9613c9712i1p223/index.html.

Walzer, Michael. "In Response: Support for Modesty and the Nation-State." *The Communitarian Network* 11, no. 2 (Spring 2001). http://www.gwu.edu/~ccps/rcq/rcq_inresponse_walzer.html.

– *Spheres of Justice: A Defense of Pluralism and Equality*. New York: Basic Books, 1983.

Wenar, Leif. "John Rawls." In *The Stanford Encyclopedia of Philosophy* edited by Edward N. Zalta. http://plato.stanford.edu/archives/win2012/entries/rawls/.

THE MACAT LIBRARY
BY DISCIPLINE

AFRICANA STUDIES

Chinua Achebe's *An Image of Africa: Racism in Conrad's Heart of Darkness*
W. E. B. Du Bois's *The Souls of Black Folk*
Zora Neale Huston's *Characteristics of Negro Expression*
Martin Luther King Jr's *Why We Can't Wait*
Toni Morrison's *Playing in the Dark: Whiteness in the American Literary Imagination*

ANTHROPOLOGY

Arjun Appadurai's *Modernity at Large: Cultural Dimensions of Globalisation*
Philippe Ariès's *Centuries of Childhood*
Franz Boas's *Race, Language and Culture*
Kim Chan & Renée Mauborgne's *Blue Ocean Strategy*
Jared Diamond's *Guns, Germs & Steel: the Fate of Human Societies*
Jared Diamond's *Collapse: How Societies Choose to Fail or Survive*
E. E. Evans-Pritchard's *Witchcraft, Oracles and Magic Among the Azande*
James Ferguson's *The Anti-Politics Machine*
Clifford Geertz's *The Interpretation of Cultures*
David Graeber's *Debt: the First 5000 Years*
Karen Ho's *Liquidated: An Ethnography of Wall Street*
Geert Hofstede's *Culture's Consequences: Comparing Values, Behaviors, Institutes and Organizations across Nations*
Claude Lévi-Strauss's *Structural Anthropology*
Jay Macleod's *Ain't No Makin' It: Aspirations and Attainment in a Low-Income Neighborhood*
Saba Mahmood's *The Politics of Piety: The Islamic Revival and the Feminist Subject*
Marcel Mauss's *The Gift*

BUSINESS

Jean Lave & Etienne Wenger's *Situated Learning*
Theodore Levitt's *Marketing Myopia*
Burton G. Malkiel's *A Random Walk Down Wall Street*
Douglas McGregor's *The Human Side of Enterprise*
Michael Porter's *Competitive Strategy: Creating and Sustaining Superior Performance*
John Kotter's *Leading Change*
C. K. Prahalad & Gary Hamel's *The Core Competence of the Corporation*

CRIMINOLOGY

Michelle Alexander's *The New Jim Crow: Mass Incarceration in the Age of Colorblindness*
Michael R. Gottfredson & Travis Hirschi's *A General Theory of Crime*
Richard Herrnstein & Charles A. Murray's *The Bell Curve: Intelligence and Class Structure in American Life*
Elizabeth Loftus's *Eyewitness Testimony*
Jay Macleod's *Ain't No Makin' It: Aspirations and Attainment in a Low-Income Neighborhood*
Philip Zimbardo's *The Lucifer Effect*

ECONOMICS

Janet Abu-Lughod's *Before European Hegemony*
Ha-Joon Chang's *Kicking Away the Ladder*
David Brion Davis's *The Problem of Slavery in the Age of Revolution*
Milton Friedman's *The Role of Monetary Policy*
Milton Friedman's *Capitalism and Freedom*
David Graeber's *Debt: the First 5000 Years*
Friedrich Hayek's *The Road to Serfdom*
Karen Ho's *Liquidated: An Ethnography of Wall Street*

John Maynard Keynes's *The General Theory of Employment, Interest and Money*
Charles P. Kindleberger's *Manias, Panics and Crashes*
Robert Lucas's *Why Doesn't Capital Flow from Rich to Poor Countries?*
Burton G. Malkiel's *A Random Walk Down Wall Street*
Thomas Robert Malthus's *An Essay on the Principle of Population*
Karl Marx's *Capital*
Thomas Piketty's *Capital in the Twenty-First Century*
Amartya Sen's *Development as Freedom*
Adam Smith's *The Wealth of Nations*
Nassim Nicholas Taleb's *The Black Swan: The Impact of the Highly Improbable*
Amos Tversky's & Daniel Kahneman's *Judgment under Uncertainty: Heuristics and Biases*
Mahbub Ul Haq's *Reflections on Human Development*
Max Weber's *The Protestant Ethic and the Spirit of Capitalism*

FEMINISM AND GENDER STUDIES

Judith Butler's *Gender Trouble*
Simone De Beauvoir's *The Second Sex*
Michel Foucault's *History of Sexuality*
Betty Friedan's *The Feminine Mystique*
Saba Mahmood's *The Politics of Piety: The Islamic Revival and the Feminist Subject*
Joan Wallach Scott's *Gender and the Politics of History*
Mary Wollstonecraft's *A Vindication of the Rights of Woman*
Virginia Woolf's *A Room of One's Own*

GEOGRAPHY

The Brundtland Report's *Our Common Future*
Rachel Carson's *Silent Spring*
Charles Darwin's *On the Origin of Species*
James Ferguson's *The Anti-Politics Machine*
Jane Jacobs's *The Death and Life of Great American Cities*
James Lovelock's *Gaia: A New Look at Life on Earth*
Amartya Sen's *Development as Freedom*
Mathis Wackernagel & William Rees's *Our Ecological Footprint*

HISTORY

Janet Abu-Lughod's *Before European Hegemony*
Benedict Anderson's *Imagined Communities*
Bernard Bailyn's *The Ideological Origins of the American Revolution*
Hanna Batatu's *The Old Social Classes And The Revolutionary Movements Of Iraq*
Christopher Browning's *Ordinary Men: Reserve Police Batallion 101 and the Final Solution in Poland*
Edmund Burke's *Reflections on the Revolution in France*
William Cronon's *Nature's Metropolis: Chicago And The Great West*
Alfred W. Crosby's *The Columbian Exchange*
Hamid Dabashi's *Iran: A People Interrupted*
David Brion Davis's *The Problem of Slavery in the Age of Revolution*
Nathalie Zemon Davis's *The Return of Martin Guerre*
Jared Diamond's *Guns, Germs & Steel: the Fate of Human Societies*
Frank Dikotter's *Mao's Great Famine*
John W Dower's *War Without Mercy: Race And Power In The Pacific War*
W. E. B. Du Bois's *The Souls of Black Folk*
Richard J. Evans's *In Defence of History*
Lucien Febvre's *The Problem of Unbelief in the 16th Century*
Sheila Fitzpatrick's *Everyday Stalinism*

Eric Foner's *Reconstruction: America's Unfinished Revolution, 1863-1877*
Michel Foucault's *Discipline and Punish*
Michel Foucault's *History of Sexuality*
Francis Fukuyama's *The End of History and the Last Man*
John Lewis Gaddis's *We Now Know: Rethinking Cold War History*
Ernest Gellner's *Nations and Nationalism*
Eugene Genovese's *Roll, Jordan, Roll: The World the Slaves Made*
Carlo Ginzburg's *The Night Battles*
Daniel Goldhagen's *Hitler's Willing Executioners*
Jack Goldstone's *Revolution and Rebellion in the Early Modern World*
Antonio Gramsci's *The Prison Notebooks*
Alexander Hamilton, John Jay & James Madison's *The Federalist Papers*
Christopher Hill's *The World Turned Upside Down*
Carole Hillenbrand's *The Crusades: Islamic Perspectives*
Thomas Hobbes's *Leviathan*
Eric Hobsbawm's *The Age Of Revolution*
John A. Hobson's *Imperialism: A Study*
Albert Hourani's *History of the Arab Peoples*
Samuel P. Huntington's *The Clash of Civilizations and the Remaking of World Order*
C. L. R. James's *The Black Jacobins*
Tony Judt's *Postwar: A History of Europe Since 1945*
Ernst Kantorowicz's *The King's Two Bodies: A Study in Medieval Political Theology*
Paul Kennedy's *The Rise and Fall of the Great Powers*
Ian Kershaw's *The "Hitler Myth": Image and Reality in the Third Reich*
John Maynard Keynes's *The General Theory of Employment, Interest and Money*
Charles P. Kindleberger's *Manias, Panics and Crashes*
Martin Luther King Jr's *Why We Can't Wait*
Henry Kissinger's *World Order: Reflections on the Character of Nations and the Course of History*
Thomas Kuhn's *The Structure of Scientific Revolutions*
Georges Lefebvre's *The Coming of the French Revolution*
John Locke's *Two Treatises of Government*
Niccolò Machiavelli's *The Prince*
Thomas Robert Malthus's *An Essay on the Principle of Population*
Mahmood Mamdani's *Citizen and Subject: Contemporary Africa And The Legacy Of Late Colonialism*
Karl Marx's *Capital*
Stanley Milgram's *Obedience to Authority*
John Stuart Mill's *On Liberty*
Thomas Paine's *Common Sense*
Thomas Paine's *Rights of Man*
Geoffrey Parker's *Global Crisis: War, Climate Change and Catastrophe in the Seventeenth Century*
Jonathan Riley-Smith's *The First Crusade and the Idea of Crusading*
Jean-Jacques Rousseau's *The Social Contract*
Joan Wallach Scott's *Gender and the Politics of History*
Theda Skocpol's *States and Social Revolutions*
Adam Smith's *The Wealth of Nations*
Timothy Snyder's *Bloodlands: Europe Between Hitler and Stalin*
Sun Tzu's *The Art of War*
Keith Thomas's *Religion and the Decline of Magic*
Thucydides's *The History of the Peloponnesian War*
Frederick Jackson Turner's *The Significance of the Frontier in American History*
Odd Arne Westad's *The Global Cold War: Third World Interventions And The Making Of Our Times*

LITERATURE

Chinua Achebe's *An Image of Africa: Racism in Conrad's Heart of Darkness*
Roland Barthes's *Mythologies*
Homi K. Bhabha's *The Location of Culture*
Judith Butler's *Gender Trouble*
Simone De Beauvoir's *The Second Sex*
Ferdinand De Saussure's *Course in General Linguistics*
T. S. Eliot's *The Sacred Wood: Essays on Poetry and Criticism*
Zora Neale Huston's *Characteristics of Negro Expression*
Toni Morrison's *Playing in the Dark: Whiteness in the American Literary Imagination*
Edward Said's *Orientalism*
Gayatri Chakravorty Spivak's *Can the Subaltern Speak?*
Mary Wollstonecraft's *A Vindication of the Rights of Women*
Virginia Woolf's *A Room of One's Own*

PHILOSOPHY

Elizabeth Anscombe's *Modern Moral Philosophy*
Hannah Arendt's *The Human Condition*
Aristotle's *Metaphysics*
Aristotle's *Nicomachean Ethics*
Edmund Gettier's *Is Justified True Belief Knowledge?*
Georg Wilhelm Friedrich Hegel's *Phenomenology of Spirit*
David Hume's *Dialogues Concerning Natural Religion*
David Hume's *The Enquiry for Human Understanding*
Immanuel Kant's *Religion within the Boundaries of Mere Reason*
Immanuel Kant's *Critique of Pure Reason*
Søren Kierkegaard's *The Sickness Unto Death*
Søren Kierkegaard's *Fear and Trembling*
C. S. Lewis's *The Abolition of Man*
Alasdair MacIntyre's *After Virtue*
Marcus Aurelius's *Meditations*
Friedrich Nietzsche's *On the Genealogy of Morality*
Friedrich Nietzsche's *Beyond Good and Evil*
Plato's *Republic*
Plato's *Symposium*
Jean-Jacques Rousseau's *The Social Contract*
Gilbert Ryle's *The Concept of Mind*
Baruch Spinoza's *Ethics*
Sun Tzu's *The Art of War*
Ludwig Wittgenstein's *Philosophical Investigations*

POLITICS

Benedict Anderson's *Imagined Communities*
Aristotle's *Politics*
Bernard Bailyn's *The Ideological Origins of the American Revolution*
Edmund Burke's *Reflections on the Revolution in France*
John C. Calhoun's *A Disquisition on Government*
Ha-Joon Chang's *Kicking Away the Ladder*
Hamid Dabashi's *Iran: A People Interrupted*
Hamid Dabashi's *Theology of Discontent: The Ideological Foundation of the Islamic Revolution in Iran*
Robert Dahl's *Democracy and its Critics*
Robert Dahl's *Who Governs?*
David Brion Davis's *The Problem of Slavery in the Age of Revolution*

Alexis De Tocqueville's *Democracy in America*
James Ferguson's *The Anti-Politics Machine*
Frank Dikotter's *Mao's Great Famine*
Sheila Fitzpatrick's *Everyday Stalinism*
Eric Foner's *Reconstruction: America's Unfinished Revolution, 1863-1877*
Milton Friedman's *Capitalism and Freedom*
Francis Fukuyama's *The End of History and the Last Man*
John Lewis Gaddis's *We Now Know: Rethinking Cold War History*
Ernest Gellner's *Nations and Nationalism*
David Graeber's *Debt: the First 5000 Years*
Antonio Gramsci's *The Prison Notebooks*
Alexander Hamilton, John Jay & James Madison's *The Federalist Papers*
Friedrich Hayek's *The Road to Serfdom*
Christopher Hill's *The World Turned Upside Down*
Thomas Hobbes's *Leviathan*
John A. Hobson's *Imperialism: A Study*
Samuel P. Huntington's *The Clash of Civilizations and the Remaking of World Order*
Tony Judt's *Postwar: A History of Europe Since 1945*
David C. Kang's *China Rising: Peace, Power and Order in East Asia*
Paul Kennedy's *The Rise and Fall of Great Powers*
Robert Keohane's *After Hegemony*
Martin Luther King Jr.'s *Why We Can't Wait*
Henry Kissinger's *World Order: Reflections on the Character of Nations and the Course of History*
John Locke's *Two Treatises of Government*
Niccolò Machiavelli's *The Prince*
Thomas Robert Malthus's *An Essay on the Principle of Population*
Mahmood Mamdani's *Citizen and Subject: Contemporary Africa And The Legacy Of Late Colonialism*
Karl Marx's *Capital*
John Stuart Mill's *On Liberty*
John Stuart Mill's *Utilitarianism*
Hans Morgenthau's *Politics Among Nations*
Thomas Paine's *Common Sense*
Thomas Paine's *Rights of Man*
Thomas Piketty's *Capital in the Twenty-First Century*
Robert D. Putman's *Bowling Alone*
John Rawls's *Theory of Justice*
Jean-Jacques Rousseau's *The Social Contract*
Theda Skocpol's *States and Social Revolutions*
Adam Smith's *The Wealth of Nations*
Sun Tzu's *The Art of War*
Henry David Thoreau's *Civil Disobedience*
Thucydides's *The History of the Peloponnesian War*
Kenneth Waltz's *Theory of International Politics*
Max Weber's *Politics as a Vocation*
Odd Arne Westad's *The Global Cold War: Third World Interventions And The Making Of Our Times*

POSTCOLONIAL STUDIES

Roland Barthes's *Mythologies*
Frantz Fanon's *Black Skin, White Masks*
Homi K. Bhabha's *The Location of Culture*
Gustavo Gutiérrez's *A Theology of Liberation*
Edward Said's *Orientalism*
Gayatri Chakravorty Spivak's *Can the Subaltern Speak?*

PSYCHOLOGY

Gordon Allport's *The Nature of Prejudice*
Alan Baddeley & Graham Hitch's *Aggression: A Social Learning Analysis*
Albert Bandura's *Aggression: A Social Learning Analysis*
Leon Festinger's *A Theory of Cognitive Dissonance*
Sigmund Freud's *The Interpretation of Dreams*
Betty Friedan's *The Feminine Mystique*
Michael R. Gottfredson & Travis Hirschi's *A General Theory of Crime*
Eric Hoffer's *The True Believer: Thoughts on the Nature of Mass Movements*
William James's *Principles of Psychology*
Elizabeth Loftus's *Eyewitness Testimony*
A. H. Maslow's *A Theory of Human Motivation*
Stanley Milgram's *Obedience to Authority*
Steven Pinker's *The Better Angels of Our Nature*
Oliver Sacks's *The Man Who Mistook His Wife For a Hat*
Richard Thaler & Cass Sunstein's *Nudge: Improving Decisions About Health, Wealth and Happiness*
Amos Tversky's *Judgment under Uncertainty: Heuristics and Biases*
Philip Zimbardo's *The Lucifer Effect*

SCIENCE

Rachel Carson's *Silent Spring*
William Cronon's *Nature's Metropolis: Chicago And The Great West*
Alfred W. Crosby's *The Columbian Exchange*
Charles Darwin's *On the Origin of Species*
Richard Dawkin's *The Selfish Gene*
Thomas Kuhn's *The Structure of Scientific Revolutions*
Geoffrey Parker's *Global Crisis: War, Climate Change and Catastrophe in the Seventeenth Century*
Mathis Wackernagel & William Rees's *Our Ecological Footprint*

SOCIOLOGY

Michelle Alexander's *The New Jim Crow: Mass Incarceration in the Age of Colorblindness*
Gordon Allport's *The Nature of Prejudice*
Albert Bandura's *Aggression: A Social Learning Analysis*
Hanna Batatu's *The Old Social Classes And The Revolutionary Movements Of Iraq*
Ha-Joon Chang's *Kicking Away the Ladder*
W. E. B. Du Bois's *The Souls of Black Folk*
Émile Durkheim's *On Suicide*
Frantz Fanon's *Black Skin, White Masks*
Frantz Fanon's *The Wretched of the Earth*
Eric Foner's *Reconstruction: America's Unfinished Revolution, 1863-1877*
Eugene Genovese's *Roll, Jordan, Roll: The World the Slaves Made*
Jack Goldstone's *Revolution and Rebellion in the Early Modern World*
Antonio Gramsci's *The Prison Notebooks*
Richard Herrnstein & Charles A Murray's *The Bell Curve: Intelligence and Class Structure in American Life*
Eric Hoffer's *The True Believer: Thoughts on the Nature of Mass Movements*
Jane Jacobs's *The Death and Life of Great American Cities*
Robert Lucas's *Why Doesn't Capital Flow from Rich to Poor Countries?*
Jay Macleod's *Ain't No Makin' It: Aspirations and Attainment in a Low Income Neighborhood*
Elaine May's *Homeward Bound: American Families in the Cold War Era*
Douglas McGregor's *The Human Side of Enterprise*
C. Wright Mills's *The Sociological Imagination*

Macat Disciplines

Access the greatest ideas and thinkers across entire disciplines, including

CRIMINOLOGY

Michelle Alexander's
The New Jim Crow: Mass Incarceration in the Age of Colorblindness

Michael R. Gottfredson & Travis Hirschi's
A General Theory of Crime

Elizabeth Loftus's
Eyewitness Testimony

Richard Herrnstein & Charles A. Murray's
The Bell Curve: Intelligence and Class Structure in American Life

Jay Macleod's
Ain't No Makin' It: Aspirations and Attainment in a Low-Income Neighborhood

Philip Zimbardo's
The Lucifer Effect

Macat analyses are available from all good bookshops and libraries.

Access hundreds of analyses through one, multimedia tool.
Join free for one month **library.macat.com**

Macat Disciplines

Access the greatest ideas and thinkers across entire disciplines, including

POSTCOLONIAL STUDIES

Roland Barthes's *Mythologies*
Frantz Fanon's *Black Skin, White Masks*
Homi K. Bhabha's *The Location of Culture*
Gustavo Gutiérrez's *A Theology of Liberation*
Edward Said's *Orientalism*
Gayatri Chakravorty Spivak's *Can the Subaltern Speak?*

Macat analyses are available from all good bookshops and libraries.

Access hundreds of analyses through one, multimedia tool.
Join free for one month **library.macat.com**

Macat Disciplines

Access the greatest ideas and thinkers across entire disciplines, including

GLOBALIZATION

Arjun Appadurai's, *Modernity at Large: Cultural Dimensions of Globalisation*

James Ferguson's, *The Anti-Politics Machine*

Geert Hofstede's, *Culture's Consequences*

Amartya Sen's, *Development as Freedom*